TITANIC

The *Titanic* leaves Belfast for her sea trials, April 2, 1912.
Public Records Office, Northern Ireland.

Titanic

THE CANADIAN STORY

Alan Hustak

Véhicule Press

Véhicule Press gratefully acknowledges the support of The Canada Council for the Arts for its publishing program.

The publisher thanks the Trustees of the National Maritime Museum, Greenwich, England for permission to print an extract from Frederic A. Hamilton's diary, and Macmillan Canada for permission to print an excerpt from *Recollections of People, Press and Politics* by Grattan O'Leary.

Cover montage and design: J.W. Stewart
Cover imaging: André Jacob
Design of chronology foldout: Justin Stahlman
Typesetting: Simon Garamond
Printing: AGMV/Marquis Inc.

CANADIAN CATALOGUING IN PUBLICATION DATA

Hustak, Alan, 1944-
Titanic : the Canadian story
ISBN 1-55065-113-7

1. Titanic (Steamship). 2. Shipwrecks North Atlantic Ocean. 3. Survival after airplane accidents, shipwrecks, etc.–Biography. I. Title.

G530.T6H88 1988   910.91634   C98-900620-4

Published by Véhicule Press
P.O.B. 125, Place du Parc Station,
Montreal, Quebec H2W 2M9

Distributed in Canada by General Distribution Services
325 Humber College, Blvd., Toronto, Ont., M9W 7C3

Distributed in the United States by LPC Group
1436 West Randolph Street, Chicago, IL 60607

Printed in Canada on alkaline paper.

To the memory of Anton Ferdinand Reit (1883-1976),
who first told me the story, his wife Anna Stephanie
Scherlowska, (1885-1958) and to their daughters Josephine,
my mother Gertrude, Helen, and my godmother Agnes.

Contents

Foreword

APRIL 1912. Pouring out of the vast reaches of Canada's northernmost frontier, smashing eastward, driving before it and dispersing the warmer early spring atmosphere, an immense mass of frigid, high pressure polar air sweeps ever further east, blanketing the northern Atlantic with its icy dome.

By Saturday, April 13, the chilly air races over Nova Scotia and hurtles across the ocean, pushing ever east and northward. By April 14, air temperatures in the high pressure's vanguard now in the vicinity of 49 degrees W. lattitude drops from the relatively mild 15°C to about 10°C by noon. During the afternoon the temperature falls steadily and by early evening it reaches 5°C, continuing to fall during the night, until by 10:30 p.m. it drops to 1°C below freezing.

Heading westward on her maiden voyage, the White Star liner *Titanic* is on a course that carries it directly into the approaching cold. At 8:40 p.m. the officer on the watch, Charles Lightholler, orders the carpenter to check the ship's fresh water supply lest it freeze. An hour or so later, the crew in the crow's nest receive a message from the bridge to keep a sharp look out for ice.

The great ship's bow cuts through the frigid waters at 21½ knots. Time passes: 10:30, 11:00, 11:30 p.m. A new day approaches. The mass of air pressure with its biting chill is not Canada's only contribution to the *Titanic*'s tragic tale.

Aboard the doomed liner are 130 men, women, and children bound for Canada. Their social and economic status are as varied as the ship's passenger manifest. Among the *Titanic*'s Canadian passengers there is a handsome sprinkling of millionaires travelling first class. In second class are merchants, salesmen of high quality goods, a chemist, a stone carver. Third class voyagers bound for Canada include, among others, a domestic in search of work, a labourer—father of seven—from Quebec City, and an aspiring Roman Catholic seminarian.

They are young, middle-aged, old; men and women of wealth and affluence, families of substance, young men pursuing their dreams, servants, domestics, a hockey player, a railroad president, a millionaire chemist. Their homes and their destinations spanned the wide Canadian country. From the shores of Nova Scotia to the cities of Quebec and Ontario, across the Great Plains of Manitoba and Saskatchewan to the rocky coast of British Columbia, the *Titanic* is remembered by descendants of the lost and saved, remembered by public monuments and private memorials.

The roles played by some of the *Titanic*'s Canadian passengers in the liner's dramatic last hours will forever be associated with the disaster: Toronto's Major Arthur Peuchen's athletically supple evacuation of the ship, the terrible error that resulted in the loss of the entire Allison family, save for the infant, Trevor Allison.

As the years pass, forgotten are the lives of *Titanic*'s Canadian passengers, even who they were. Canadians constituted one of the largest national blocs aboard the ship. An appreciable number of them were men of prominence and renown. Yet over the years their stories have faded to the point of near insignificance.

To most readers, Canada's only connection to the disaster relates principally to Halifax, Nova Scotia, where the bodies of many of the victims are buried. Forgotten is the fact that Montreal is where the second largest number of the *Titanic*'s victims are buried. Forgotten too, are the many Canadian families who were so closely associated with the disaster.

In this meticulously researched book, Alan Hustak has brought an end to the decades old oversight and neglect of Canada's *Titanic* passengers and their importance in the awesome story. The story of the *Titanic* is like an immense jigsaw puzzle whose tiny pieces are painstakingly fitted one to another until large sections appear, which in turn, are assembled to reveal major areas of the never-completed canvas.

In this book, Alan Hustak has furnished the pieces for a significant, and hitherto, largely forgotten segment of the disaster.

In the past, Canada contributed weather and ice and passengers to the *Titanic*'s story. It now provides a distinctive book.

John P. Eaton, Cold Spring, N.Y.
June 1998

Preface

THIS BOOK tells the familiar story of the *Titanic*, from a Canadian perspective. It is the untold saga of the 130 passengers who were bound for Canada aboard the ill-fated luxury liner. Among the 1,320 passengers there was a large contingent from Montreal and Winnipeg, and people from Calgary, Toronto, Vancouver, and Halifax. With few exceptions, the stories of the Canadians on board have not been reported—either overlooked or ignored by American and British authors who have written about the disaster. Of the 130 aboard, 82 died and 48 survived.

In 1992, long before James Cameron's blockbuster movie, I wrote a newspaper article for the Montreal *Gazette* about the Montrealers who were aboard the *Titanic*, to commemorate the 80th anniversary of the sinking. *Titanic: The Canadian Story* grew out of that article. Even then, interest in the story was so positive that I was taken aback. I received letters, telephone calls, and tips from readers who either knew more than I did about these people or wanted to know more. I stumbled into a hobby—whenever I travelled, I would drop into the local library to see if the city or town I was visiting had a *Titanic* connection. I talked to relatives and descendants of passengers who sailed on the *Titanic*'s maiden voyage. Eventually I found myself with a trunk full of true stories that had never been told.

This book tells the Canadian story. The *Titanic* story is really about people: those who sailed on the ship, those who died, and those who survived. The conversations quoted are taken directly from newspaper accounts, court transcripts, oral histories, official testimony, relevant letters, and diaries.

Resurrecting lost lives eight decades after an event involves a certain amount of intuition, educated guesswork, and often just plain common sense. The information is sometimes contradictory. I have had to order events to tell the tale—everything in the book happened, but perhaps not exactly the way the book says it happened.

No one can claim to be the ultimate *Titanic* expert. Everyone who navigates these waters learns something about the story, but no one will ever have all the answers. Even the most ardent enthusiast sometimes gets things wrong. There is a prominent American writer who built an essay around the fact that there were no black passengers aboard. The truth is that Joseph Laroche, his wife, and daughter Louise were on board on their way to Haiti. Some books insist the *Titanic*'s last victim, found in a lifeboat a month after the disaster, was from New Jersey; others say he was from Chicago. In fact, he was Thomson Beattie from Winnipeg. When I began my research in 1989 I asked one prominent *Titanic* historian for a list of Canadian-bound passengers, I was told "Canadians didn't exist in 1912; they were all listed as British, so no one knew who the Canadians were."

The expert was wrong.

I hope this book contributes something new to the canon and stimulates others to dig deeper and unearth stories of their own.

My interest in the *Titanic* began almost fifty years ago when my grandfather took me to an estate auction and I bought a box of books for a quarter. In it was Logan Marshall's classic, *The Sinking of the Titanic and Great Sea Disasters* published in 1912. I still have it. I read it and was captivated. Then I saw the movie with Barbara Stanwyck and Clifton Webb in 1953. I was hooked.

Why does this story have such enduring appeal? It should have been eclipsed by World War I, the sinking of the *Empress of Ireland*, the *Lusitania*, and the Halifax Explosion. But it wasn't. It is a drama which played out in two hours and forty minutes and its players numbered 2,228. Even more important, it is a story about souls, both lost and saved. It is about vices and virtues—arrogance, cowardice, sacrifice, and nobility. In a commentary for Vision TV's "Skylight," broadcaster and *Titanic* psychoanalyst Tim Wilson succinctly described it as a story that "religiously reminds us that our fate is in the hands of a power larger than our own. It flings in our faces the huge question, both physical and metaphysical: knowing you have an hour or less, how will you face your death? What will you give up and what will you hold on to? It's the power of that question that makes the legend of the *Titanic*, even more than the great ship itself, unsinkable."

I must thank Michael Cooke, former assistant managing editor of the *Gazette* in Montreal for initially allowing me to run with the idea. The manuscript, however, is as much John P. Eaton's—a leading *Titanic* authority—as it is mine. He has been an enthusiastic supporter since I first wrote to him for assistance ten years ago. He has since become a valued friend who answers my telephone calls at all hours of the day. Without his generosity, wit, and patience, and his willingness to share with me his encyclopedic knowledge about the disaster I would have literally been at sea. I am also indebted to Charles Haas and Michael Findlay, officers of Titanic International, for their invaluable assistance, and to Geoffrey E. Whitfield, and Brian J. Ticehurst at the British Titanic Society. Pamela Clark, deputy registrar of the Royal Archives at Windsor and Charles Kidd, editor of Debrett's Peerage Limited, contributed as did Mort Van Ostrand, Brian Meister, Bob Stevens, and Ian Easterbrook. I also appreciate the kindness of Peter Brett in Nova Scotia and his mother, Mrs. Flora Brett in Winnipeg who provided remarkable first-hand recollections about the Fortune family. Thanks as well to William Fong, Ella Deeks, Rose Clothier, Betty Vanden Bosch, John Baxter and his wife, Herman De Wulf, Orian B. Hallor, and Alice Solomonian. Hugh Brewster's article on Major Peuchen in *Toronto Life* was also helpful, as were Stephen T. Molson, Beatrice Lacon, and Sandra Gwyn. David Zeni and Stephan Jönsson also gave me useful information. Then there are the archivists and librarians across the country: Maureen Hoogenraad at the National Archives of Canada; Gary Shutlak, senior archivist at Nova Scotia Archives and Records Management; and Clive Powell, Maritime Museum, Greenwich; Bishop's College School archives; Sheryl Lynch at the Halifax City Regional Library; Annie Kolzar, special collections department at the Hamilton Public Library; Lindsay Moir at the Glenbow Alberta Archives; Elizabeth Blight at the Manitoba Provincial Archives; Joyce Playford, at the Moose Jaw Public Library; Mary Smith, curator of St. Mary's District Museum (Ontario); Mary Jambor in Winnipeg City Clerk's department; Stephen Lyons, at Canadian Pacific Archives;and Maxine Corea at the Wellington County Museum and Archives.

The assistance of Louise Duchastel-Fleischman, Bob Bracken, Gilda van Norman, Tim Wilson, Gavin Murphy, Ross Mackay, Alan Ruffman of Geomarine Associates in Halifax, Betty Rollins, Bob Knuckle, Mae Morrison, Robert G. Ramsey, Stéphane Lajoie-Plante, and Donald Lynch of the Titanic Historical Society is also appreciated. As always, special thanks go to Johanne Norchet for help in translation, Tony Harpes for his enthralling contribution, and to *Gazette* librarians Agnes McFarlane, Michael Porritt, and Donna McHutchin.

I am especially indebted, once again to Simon Dardick and Véhicule for taking the manuscript, to Vicki Marcok, and to Nancy Marrelli who edited it.

Montreal June 1998

AMDG

Alice Fortune of Winnipeg.
"I am a dangerous person to travel with."
Courtesy of Flora Brett.

Chapter One

ONLY AFTER THE CATASTROPHE was Alice Fortune able to appreciate the clairvoyant's warning. The heat in Cairo that February day in 1912 was so stifling that she left her suite in Shepheard's Hotel to sit in the shade on the veranda overlooking the Nile. The hotel was one of the city's most famous landmarks. It had a Moorish hall lit by a glass dome, and a ballroom with lotus pillars modelled on those at Karnak. The veranda café was crowded with wicker chairs and tables overlooking the Midian Opéra, the main public square. Shepheard's was the giddy social centre of British Cairo and the watering hole of its moneyed classes. As Alice sat down, a wrinkled man with a fez beckoned to her through the balustrade. As she approached, he took her hand and examined her palm.

"You are in danger every time you travel on the sea, for I see you adrift on the ocean in an open boat," he said. "You will lose everything but your life."

William Sloper was there when it happened and in his memoirs he tells us Alice gave the soothsayer some money and the little man disappeared into the teeming crowd, "into the obscurity from which he so briefly emerged."

Alice was just twenty-four and still under her parents' wing. She was not superstitious nor easily intimidated. Still, she seemed ill at ease as she fingered the string of cultured pearls she always wore around her slim, elegant neck. She wasn't frightened by the prediction but vaguely concerned for her family. She had come with her father, mother, two sisters, and her younger brother halfway across the world from Winnipeg, Manitoba, to see the Great Pyramid of Cheops, the monumental Sphinx, and the treasures in the Museum of Antiquities.

Alice was very much her father's daughter—vivacious, carefree, stubborn, and self-assured. For her to share her concern would be out of character. Her father, Mark Fortune, was a self-made man with a bank account that matched the family name. Lured to California by inflated dreams when he was still a teenager, he left Wentworth, Ontario, where he was born in 1847, and spent two years in San Francisco. In 1871 he was in the right place at the right time when he arrived in Manitoba at the end of the first Riel Rebellion. Led by Louis Riel, a group of disgruntled Métis had sought provincial status to improve conditions in their isolated colony. When their grievances were ignored they took up arms against the Canadian government. Their rebellion, poorly planned, was quickly crushed. The vanquished Métis were ordered by law from the very land they had sought to protect. Mark Fortune snapped up a thousand acres along the Assiniboine River. A few years later Winnipeg's main thoroughfare, Portage Avenue, was surveyed through his property, and by the time he was thirty, he was a rich man. He married Mary McDougald, a girl from Portage la Prairie, and they had six children: Robert, Clara, Ethel, Mabel, Alice, and Charles. Along the way Fortune was elected a Winnipeg city councillor and was a trustee of Knox Presbyterian Church. His contemporaries remembered him as brash and self-confident, "probably the most expert of Winnipeg's curlers. His judgement was sound, his discrimination keen, his life purpose high."

In 1911 Fortune built a substantial thirty-six-room Tudor-style mansion which, although now converted into condominiums, still stands at 393 Wellington Crescent in Winnipeg's finest neighbourhood. The same year, his youngest son, Charles, a vigorous and handsome eighteen-year-old with sandy hair, blue eyes, and a serious face, graduated from Bishop's College School in Lennoxville, Quebec, with citations for academic and athletic excellence. His father had waited for Charles to finish school before rewarding the entire family by "finishing them off," with the ultimate mark of breeding, a Grand Tour of Europe. By then, his two eldest children, Robert and Clara, had made lives of their own in British Columbia, and they didn't want to go.

The second Fortune daughter, Ethel, had already announced her engagement to a rising Toronto banker, Crawford Gordon. Her friends remember Ethel as one of those headstrong personalities who sets her own goals then vigorously pursues them. But she agreed to postpone her wedding to shop for a trousseau in Europe and chaperone her younger siblings.

Mabel Fortune moved in an orbit of her own. Blithe, unselfconscious, and a little high-strung, she was attractive but spoiled. Much to her parents dismay Mabel had fallen in love with Harrison Driscoll, a jazz musician from Minnesota. The Fortunes thought they could stifle the romance, or at least cool her ardour, by taking her away for several months.

The Fortunes were part of a smug and complacent crowd with an imperial perspective of the world. They were born during the reign of Queen Victoria. Canadians were part of the British Empire and all that it entailed. It was said that "Canada was a favoured daughter in her mother's house, but mistress in her own." Canadians took exceptional pride in the fact that their head of state, the Governor General, Prince Arthur—the Duke of Connaught—was the queen's youngest son. Jan Morris describes the time in her trilogy, *Pax Britannica*: "There was hardly a moment of the day, hardly a facet of daily living in which the fact of Empire was not emphasized. From exhortatory editorials to matchbox lids, from children's fashion to parlour games, from music hall lyrics to parish church sermons, the Imperial Theme was relentlessly drummed." Rich Canadians in foreign lands considered themselves first and foremost as British subjects. Everyone else was regarded as a quaint extra in a drama directed by the Empire and produced for its benefit. Even French Canadians accepted their colonial status and generally applauded the notion put forward by one politician that Quebecers were "good, loyal and faithful British subjects: Englishmen but with one difference—they speak French."

It was a time of transatlantic travel when twenty pieces of hold luggage were the absolute minimum for social survival in First Class. Gentlemen were expected to change clothes four times a day. Mark Fortune was willing to respect the conventions but he never went anywhere without his matted and moth-eaten Winnipeg Buffalo Coat. He had had it for years and considered the heavy fur coat something of a good luck charm, a talisman. His wife tried to talk him out of packing so useless a garment on a trip to Egypt, but he wouldn't listen. "You never know when it might come in handy," he said as he stashed the coat into a steamer trunk.

In the first decade of the twentieth century, only a few privileged Canadians could afford to sail off to Europe for the winter, and it seemed that those who did all knew one another.

Making the trip with the Fortunes were three well-heeled Winnipeg bachelors: realtor Thomson Beattie, Beattie's best friend and Union Bank President Thomas McCaffry, who had recently been transferred to Vancouver, and John Hugo Ross, the son of Arthur Wellington Ross, the Liberal-Conservative Member of Parliament for the Manitoba riding of Lisgar. John Hugo was born in Glengarry, Ontario, in 1875, but his parents moved to Winnipeg when he was two, where his father became one of the largest real estate brokers in the province. Ross Sr. became involved in the building of the CPR, and in 1878 was elected a member of the Manitoba legislature. He resigned his seat in the legislature and in 1882 was elected to the House of Commons for the first time. As a child, John Hugo was described as "a rosy faced boy in knickerbockers, riding his dog sled or off skating. On Sunday and special occasions he was the little gentleman in a kilt." When he was still in his teens his father got him a position at the vice-regal residence, Liberty Hall, as secretary to Lieutenant Governor James Coolebrook Patterson. He worked there for a year, then in 1896 he left Winnipeg for Toronto where he went into business for himself as a mining broker. He squandered his money, the firm failed, and he had a falling out with his father. In 1902, with twenty-five cents in his pocket, he left for the Klondike to pan for gold. He soon realized the Rush was over. Then his father died. He inherited the business and returned to Winnipeg to look after his widowed mother. Dapper and flamboyant, Ross had a sarcastic wit. He and realtor Thomson Beattie had offices across the hall from each other in the same Merchants Bank Building.

Thomson Beattie had been born late in his mother's life, in Fergus,

Ontario, on November 27, 1875, in a large Victorian farmhouse known as Belleside. The last of eleven children in a solid Presbyterian family, he was twenty-four years younger than his eldest brother, William. His mother, Janet Wilson, had been born to Scottish immigrant parents on May 15, 1830 aboard the *Justinian* in the mid-Atlantic—a ship bound for Canada. The Wilsons settled in Fergus, a small but thriving industrial community fifty kilometres west of Toronto where Janet grew up. In 1850, she married banker John Beattie who had worked as an agent for the Royal Bank before he opened his own bank. In 1871, he was named clerk of Wellington County, a position he held until he died twenty-three years later.

Their youngest son, Thomson, was a precious child, a shy, dreamy boy who was close to his mother. He apprenticed in his father's bank where he was programmed to become an accountant. But when his father died in 1897, Thomson and another brother, Charles, took their share of the estate and moved to Winnipeg. By then the city was the commercial distribution centre for all of Western Canada, "the clearing house for everything west of the Lakehead," and it was able to boast that it was home to more millionaires per capita than any other city in North America. In Winnipeg, Beattie teamed up with another young, resourceful, and determined Scot, Richard Waugh. Together they took over the Haslam Land Company, and within five years their enterprise was so successful that Beattie was able to buy a large house that he shared with a medical doctor in Fort Rouge at 560 River Avenue, a prosperous residential neighbourhood a few blocks from the Fortune family mansion. Richard Waugh was elected mayor of Winnipeg in 1911, and Beattie was left to run the business by himself. He didn't display a high profile in the community but was generous in support of civic causes. "His cheque book was always at the command of any worthy charity," a colleague recalled, "and there is not a charitable institution in the city but has been made the richer through his generosity."

Beattie was a prominent member of Winnipeg's bachelor subculture. It was often said "that he was of such a retiring disposition that little was known of him except by his most intimate friends." The person who knew him best was Thomas McCaffry. Beattie and McCaffry resembled each other, dressed alike, and were often mistaken for brothers. The *Winnipeg Free Press* remarked on how similar they were, and observed the two of them "were almost inseparable." McCaffry, a forty-six year old banker was born in Ireland, but grew up in Trois-Rivières and Montreal before he was transferred to Winnipeg. He and Beattie often vacationed together. In 1908 they went to the Aegean and in 1910 to North Africa. They spent a lot of time in each other's company, but they were not without female admirers. Maud MacArthur, a stenographer who worked in Ross' office was drawn towards Thomson Beattie in a way she could not articulate until he was gone.

The Fortunes and the Winnipeg Musketeers—Beattie, McCaffry, and Ross, left Winnipeg by train on January 8, 1912, and on January 20 sailed from New York aboard the Cunard liner *Franconia* bound for Trieste, main seaport of the Austro-Hungarian Empire. Aboard ship they met William Sloper, a footloose, affable young man from New Britain, Connecticut, who was so smitten with Alice Fortune, that he attached himself to their party. He was twenty-eight, and rich enough to do whatever he pleased because his father owned a Boston bank. Mrs. Fortune liked Sloper, but Mark Fortune didn't think he was strong willed enough to be a match for his daughter. They were at sea sixteen days, stopping along the way at Algiers, Monaco, and Athens before they disembarked. From Trieste they made their way by train down the Adriatic Coast, through Greece, then across the Mediterranean to Jerusalem before going on to Egypt. They posed for snapshots in front of the Karnak Temple at Luxor. Beattie sent copies of the photographs to his brother Fred in Vancouver. Mark Fortune, McCaffry, and Ross are all sporting keffiyeh, the traditional Arab headgear. Other photos show them feeding the pigeons in St. Mark's Square in Venice. By that time, at the end of March, Ross was feeling ill and Beattie, too, was exhausted from their travels. Both were weary and anxious to get home. They said as much in one postcard to friends in Winnipeg. "We are on the last lap of doing the old lands and ready for Winnipeg and business." The Fortunes were also weary and had had enough of sightseeing. When they

"We are changing ships and coming home in a new, unsinkable boat."

(From left to right) Hugo Ross, unidentified companion, Thomas
McCaffry, Mark Fortune, and Thomson Beattie, feeding the
pigeons in St. Mark's Square, Venice, March 1912.
Courtesy of Mrs. Jack Tweddle.

reached Paris they cancelled their plans to sail home later on the *Mauretania* and decided to book passage on the maiden voyage of a celebrated new ship. Fortune booked three outside cabins for his family, C-22, 24, and 26. Ross took an inside cabin, A-10, and McCaffry and Beattie a forward cabin, C-6. "We are changing ships and coming home in a new, unsinkable boat," Beattie wrote to his mother in Fergus.

They crossed to London and ended their vacation with a bon voyage party on Easter Sunday at the Carlton Hotel. The Fortune sisters appeared for dinner in their new Worth gowns from Paris, in the popular colour that spring, Primrose Pink. All three wore their pearl chokers which had been made fashionable by the dowager Queen mother, Alexandra. As they were walking through the Palm Court on their way to dinner, Alice spotted her old friend, William Sloper, standing alone at the top of the staircase. They hadn't seen each other since they had been in Egypt together. She invited him to join the family for dinner.

"One of the first questions Alice asked me was 'when are you going home?'" Sloper wrote in his memoirs. Only the day before he had made reservations to sail back to America aboard the Cunard liner *Mauretania*, which was then the fastest ship afloat. Sloper was so beguiled by Alice he impulsively decided to change his travel plans so he could be with her. "Alice was a very pretty girl and an excellent dancing partner. If that were not enough inducement, her assurance that she knew of twenty people who would be passengers with us, who had been on our steamer in January going to Europe, settled it," he wrote later.

He exchanged his tickets on Monday, and when he surprised Alice with the news, she flirted with him.

"I am sorry you did it. Haven't you forgotten? I am a dangerous person to travel with. Don't you remember the fortune teller last winter on the terrace at Shepheard's Hotel?"

"That fortune teller told every American tourist the same thing," Sloper grinned.

The following morning, April 10, 1912, Sloper joined the Fortunes, Ross, Beattie, and McCaffry, and took the boat train to Southampton. Ross was now so ill with dysentery that he had to be carried to his compartment on a stretcher. Sick as he was, he was determined to get home. He was not going to miss the maiden voyage of the world's largest steamship, the White Star Line's majestic Royal Mail Ship, *Titanic*.

Chapter Two

THE *Titanic* was a technical dream, secure and serene. It was the largest ship afloat and it was built by William James, first Lord Pirrie, who was born in Quebec City on May 31,1874. Pirrie's roots, however, were in Belfast. He was one year old when his immigrant father died and his mother took him back to Ireland. Until his own death at sea in 1921, Pirrie carried with him a book of pithy inspirational sayings she had written for him, Proverbs such as "stay late to finish early," or "it is better to accomplish a small amount of work than to half-do ten times as much." His own personal favourite: "In small beginnings are great labours born." A domineering man with no formal education, Pirrie went to work as a draughtsman in Belfast at the Harland and Wolff shipbuilding company when he was fifteen. By the time he was twenty-seven he was a full partner. Innovative, obstinate, and impatient with delay, he knew every part of the business as well as any employee. He was twice elected mayor of Belfast, in 1896 and 1897. The American journalist William T. Stead, who was aboard the *Titanic* on its maiden voyage, called Pirrie "the greatest shipbuilder whom the world has ever seen. He has built more ships and bigger ships than any man since the days of Noah. And he not only builds ships, but he owns them, directs them, and controls them on all the seas of the world."

That was something of an overstatement. Although White Star ships were of British registry, the line itself was owned not by Pirrie, but by one of the world's first multi-national corporations, the International Mercantile Marine Company (IMM), which was financed by American banker J. Pierpoint Morgan. Although the line's head office was in London, eight of its thirteen directors were American financeers. IMM wanted to monopolize transatlantic passenger service but when it tried to buy the rival British-owned Cunard line, Morgan discovered British pride was not for sale. He offered shareholders 80 percent more than what Cunard was worth, but was turned down. Terry Coleman offered a succinct explanation in his book, *The Liners*: "The legal position was and is this: A ship is not an ordinary piece of property to be bought and sold. A ship is, in the eyes of British law, a piece of the realm which happens to be at sea. To maintain jurisdiction over this travelling territory, it is necessary that it be owned by British nationals."

When Morgan's attempt to buy Cunard failed, he teamed up with the managing director of the White Star Line, Bruce Ismay, and with Pirrie, who was on the board of directors of both IMM and the White Star Line, to finance a challenge. Over dinner one night in 1907 they came up with a scheme to build two ships larger than anything afloat. They imagined vessels so luxurious and beautiful the sea goddess Amphitrite would pale with envy. They would be in a class by themselves, so huge that no dry dock, berth, or pier large enough to accommodate them had yet been built.

Ismay accepted a suggestion from a U.S. consular official in Siam, of all places, that the ships be named *Olympic* and *Titanic*. The *Olympic* was launched in 1907, and when it left on its maiden voyage it was the largest ship afloat. It performed so well, a third ship, *Gigantic*, was planned even before the second was completed. On March 31, 1909, the *Titanic*'s keel was laid, and it was launched on May 31, 1911. It was the second ship to bear the name *Titanic*. According to Lloyd's register the first ship by that name was built in 1888 for Smith & Service. It was not the most auspicious name for a vessel. In Greek mythology the Titans deposed their father as ruler of the universe and were in turn deposed by the Olympians who consigned the Titans to Tartaurus, a classical netherworld even worse than hell. The first *Titanic* was 280 feet long and was twice damaged by fire and ran aground near Bangor, Maine, in 1900. It was sold shortly after and its name was changed to the *Luis Alberto*.

Mae Morrison's father worked on the *Titanic*, and as a teenager growing up in Belfast she watched it being built from the front bedroom window of her family's house. Morrison, who later lived in Pointe Claire, Quebec, remembered they rushed to finish the ship. "They worked on Sundays. That just wasn't done in good Presbyterian families in those days. On one of the last Sundays of March 1912, my father came round and said we were allowed to go aboard for a visit. The families of the men who worked round the clock at the shipyard fitting her out were invited, but my mother wouldn't go."

"Mother was a lovely lady, but a wee bit too prim," Morrison explained, "She said to my father, 'No good will come from working on the Lord's Day. So my father took me and some girlfriends to see the ship. It was beyond me. The grandest thing I ever saw. Grander than a grand hotel. Mirrors everywhere. I remember the mirrors and the green carpets and all the oak. Gorgeous. All those mirrors."

There is an ominous painting by Charles Dixon in the Ulster Transport Museum, *The Titanic Fitting Out*. The canvas depicts a night scene and the work is dark and alarming. What is supposed to be a picture of a great ship's joyous debut is instead black and filled with prophetic menace. Yet seen in daylight, the 46,300 tonne vessel was magnificent—882 feet long and almost eleven storeys tall.

A stroll up the ship's cascading main staircase, with its hand-carved oak balustrades, led passengers past a large decorative panel inset with a clock and carved with allegorical figures representing Honour and Glory crowning time. At the top of the staircase on A Deck a long corridor bordered the reading and writing room and opened into the elegant First Class Lounge. Decorated in pastel green with a soft shade of pink known as Rose de Berri, the room was appointed with walnut furnishings and Aubusson tapestries. Further aft, off limits to female passengers, was the Men's Smoking Lounge. The vast room, 65 feet long, was panelled in mahogany inlaid with mother of pearl. It had stained glass windows and an open fireplace. On either side of the bar, beyond the lounge, were two verandah palm courts with unobstructed views of the sea. The ship's first class staterooms and cabins were in a variety of architectural styles: Louis XIV, XV, XVI, Empire, Italian Renaissance, Regency, and Queen Anne. A dining room on D Deck at the foot of the grand staircase was modelled on Haddon Hall, a seventeenth century English manor house in Hatfield. There was a 30 foot swimming pool on the starboard side of F Deck and a Turkish Bath appointed with tiled walls, gilt beams, and carved teak stanchions.

With fifteen watertight bulkheads and a double hull, the *Titanic* was considered so technologically advanced it couldn't sink. No one actually pronounced it unsinkable, but the impression was widespread. The *Gazette* in Montreal for example, believed it to be "a triumph of the designers and the builders' craft. Every precaution was taken to make it as safe as it was great. Travellers went aboard with the confidence that they would reach their destination as if they were stepping upon a train on a well managed railway."

Because of the overwhelming sense of security, the *Titanic* carried only sixteen lifeboats and four collapsible Englehart rafts which together could theoretically accommodate 1,178 people—about one third of all the people it could carry. Given the experience at the time, the oversight was not as irresponsible as it first appears. The invention of the wireless gave passengers a false sense of security. Before Marconi, ships vanished without a trace. Now, according to the theory, all a ship in distress had to do was send out a signal and be rescued. Since Atlantic shipping lanes were always crowded, no vessel was more than two or three hours away from another, close enough to respond to a call for help. The odds of being killed in a White Star ship were calculated at one million to one. Since the invention of the wireless, White Star had ferried more than two million passengers across the Atlantic, and lost only two when the *Republic* and the *Florida* collided on January 24, 1909. Finally, because the *Titanic* was so huge and could remain afloat with as many as five of her watertight compartments flooded, the conventional wisdom was that the ship could stay afloat for days, or at least long enough for every passenger to be rescued by passing ships. Even then the travelling public recognized the inherent risk. Lifeboats for everyone did not guarantee the personal safety of each and every passenger. Regulations drafted by the British Board of Trade in 1894 required the White Star Line to provide lifeboats for 962 people. The regulations had been drafted when the largest ship afloat was 10,000 tonnes. *Titanic* was four times as big, but the same outdated rules applied.

J. P. Morgan was supposed to be on the *Titanic*'s maiden voyage, but business interests kept him from sailing. He had been booked into one of two so-called "Millionaires Suites" B-52-54-56, with its own private promenade. The accommodation was eventually turned over to the White Star Line's managing director, J. Bruce Ismay. The adjoining suite of rooms, B 58-60 was occupied by the Baxter family from Montreal. If Hollywood producer James Cameron had wanted to create a real-life, ill-fated shipboard romance when he made his epic 1998 blockbuster, *Titanic*, the affair between twenty-four-year-old Quigg Baxter and a Belgian courtesan, Berthe Antoine Mayné, had the makings of a quintessential love story.

The Baxters' staterooms amidship were among the few to be photographed so we know what the accommodations looked like. We also know the family paid 247 pounds, ten shillings and five pence for their tickets, the equivalent of about $135,000 in today's money. Yet little is known about the Montrealers who occupied the rooms. Perhaps it is because, in spite of their Irish name, they were French-speaking and didn't leave any lasting impression on their fellow passengers. Or, perhaps they have been deliberately ignored because even though they had money they were considered social climbers who just didn't belong.

There were three in the Baxter party: Hélène de Lanaudière-Chaput Baxter, a fifty-year-old widow returning to Canada with her doe-eyed, twenty-seven-year-old daughter, Mary Hélène Douglas, and her youngest son, Quigg.

Mrs. Baxter's husband, James "Diamond Jim" Baxter, was born in Ontario's Middlesex County, one of eleven children in a family of so- called Black Irish immigrants. As a young man he moved to Montreal where he went to work as a jeweller. Persuasive and charming, with a genius for shady deals, he opened a suite of offices in 1877 in the heart of the city's financial district, at 120 St. François Xavier Street. Thirteen years later the *Dominion Illustrated* reported he was running "a general brokerage business such as negotiating loans, buying, selling or exchanging real estate,

Hélène Baxter and daughter Mary Hélène (Zette) at the
family cottage, Senneville, Quebec, 1911.
Courtesy of John Baxter.

Quigg Baxter, Lac St-Louis, Quebec, 1911.
Courtesy of John Baxter.

buying commercial paper, making advances on warehouse receipts, and in short, everything that legitimately comes under these headings. By his zeal, energy, enterprise, rare executive ability and integrity, he has drawn about him a wide and steadily increasing circle of high class patrons."

His marriage in August 1882 to de Lanaudière-Chaput, twenty years his junior, allowed him entry into Quebec's close-knit French-speaking community. His wife, after all, was able to claim the fabled heroine, Madeleine de Verchères as an ancestor. According to the legend, in 1692, when Verchères was only fourteen, she tricked a raiding party of Iroquois Indians into believing an unarmed stockade was heavily guarded. The Indians fled, a massacre was avoided, and the district just east of Montreal was able to flourish. Her descendants were given title to an entire county that still bears the family name Lanaudière.

Baxter moved his bride into a huge though unremarkable house on the corner of Sherbrooke Street at Drummond, number 1201. The mansion, since dismantled and rebuilt stone by stone, still stands kitty-corner to the Ritz-Carlton Hotel on Sherbrooke street and for many years was the corporate headquarters for Corby Distillers Ltd. When the Baxters lived there the mansion stood in the centre of an exclusive residential district known as the Square Mile, an enclave of rich and titled families, who at the time controlled 70 percent of Canada's wealth.

Because the Baxters were Irish, Catholic, and French-speaking, they were not considered part of the social order of the old moneyed Scottish Presbyterians who built the neighbourhood. Race and culture separated Montrealers at the turn of the century as deeply as religion. In spite of their wealth, the Baxters were social outsiders.

Their next-door neighbour was William Cornelius Van Horne, head of the Canadian Pacific Railway; Baron Mount Stephen lived in a mansion one block below. Up the hill stood Ravenscrag, the estate of shipping magnate Sir Montague Allan, head of the Allan Royal Mail Line's fleet of steamships.

The Baxter's first son, baptized Anthony William, but called James, was born in 1883. A daughter, christened Mary Hélène, but nicknamed

Zette, was born two years later. Their youngest son, Quigg Edmond, was born in 1887. The product of two cultures, the Baxter children were raised to speak English to their father and French to their mother, and even as youngsters, were proficient in both languages.

Quigg was educated by the Jesuits at Loyola, a private boys' school in Montreal. As a teenager he joined the Montreal Amateur Athletic Association and quickly earned a reputation as a star football and hockey player.

In 1892, his father built the Baxter Block, an ambitious development on St. Lawrence Boulevard just south of Pine Avenue that put twenty-eight stores under a single roof in what might be described as Canada's first shopping mall. By 1899, a promotional business publication, *Men in Canada*, described Baxter as "the largest private banker in Canada," and a philanthropist who "devoted a large share of his accumulated wealth to improve the outlying districts of Montreal."

The family's reputation fell apart the following year when Baxter was accused by the U.S. Department of Revenue of violating currency exchange regulations. Because he was a Canadian, Baxter wasn't prosecuted. But in 1900 he was charged and convicted of defrauding his Bank of Ville Marie of more than $40,000, the equivalent of $1.2 million in today's purchasing power.

He was sentenced to five years in prison and he died shortly after he was parolled in 1905, three weeks shy of his sixty-sixth birthday. His obituary in the *Montreal Star* reported that "After his release he was soon seen upon the streets. He opened a diamond and financial brokerage in the Baxter Block and with the collection of his rents, kept himself employed up to the time of his death. For many years Mr. Baxter was generally reputed to be very wealthy," the *Star* continued, "But later on when his affairs reached a crisis, it was found that a great share of this reported wealth had disappeared or never really existed after all, it is hard to say which."

The newspaper was wrong.

The family's circumstances may have been diminished by his death, but financially it was far from down. Baxter had stashed money in France,

Switzerland, and Belgium and his investments enabled his widow to move into a comfortable brownstone at a still-respectable address on the border of the Square Mile, at 33 St. Famille Street, close to the McGill University campus. She began a routine that required her to go abroad each year to look after her investments. Each autumn as the social season began in Montreal, she would leave, to spend the winter in France, and return to Canada in the spring just as the season ended. She sold the Baxter Block in November 1911, and left for Paris. Quigg, the apple of his mother's eye, dropped out of his first term in Applied Science at McGill to go with her. By then it seemed the young man was well on the way to redeeming the family's tarnished name.

Handsome in spite of a scarred face and lopsided grin, he had already distinguished himself as a member of the Montreal Shamrocks Hockey Team. However, during a game early in 1907, he caught a low blow from a stick in his left eye and lost the sight in it. Although he was no longer able to play the game, he went on to coach. He is credited with organizing one of the first international hockey tournaments ever played in Paris.

It was Quigg who introduced his sister Zette to her future husband, Fred Charles Douglas, the doctor who treated him for his eye injuries. They were married in 1909, and the Douglases moved into the house on St. Famille Street. Living with his mother-in-law strained the marriage. The couple went to London in 1910 so that he could do his post graduate studies, but Mrs. Baxter followed. When Douglas returned to Montreal he opened his own public health clinic in an office at 51 Park Avenue.

In the spring of 1912, Zette left him to his practice and went off to join her mother and her brother in Paris where she celebrated her twenty-seventh birthday.

Eager to make an impression back home, they chose to sail on the *Titanic*.

Travelling with Quigg was a mysterious woman identified only as a "Mrs. B. de Villiers." Her real name was Berthe Mayné, a twenty-four-year-old cabaret singer and courtesan who had a liaison with a French soldier from the Belgian Congo, Fernand de Villiers. When de Villiers left

Bert and Vera Dick of Calgary were married the day the *Titanic*
was launched, May 31, 1911.
Courtesy of Gilda van Norman.

her to go to the Belgian Congo, she adopted the name as a stage name. She also sang in Paris under the stage name Bella Vielly. The Belgian newspaper, *Nieuws*, described her as being "well known in Brussels in circles of pleasure and was often seen in the company of people who liked to wine and dine and enjoy life." From the moment Quigg met her, their affair was torrid, passionate, and secret. It is not clear whether Baxter had proposed and was bringing Mayné to Canada so they could be married, or whether the trip was meant to be nothing more than an extended fling for the two lovers. For the sake of appearance, Mayné had a cabin of her own, C-90, one deck below, conveniently located just off the First Class entrance stairwell, with discreet access to the Promenade Deck.

Lord Pirrie was himself scheduled to be on board, but he needed prostate surgery, and he too cancelled. In his place he sent his nephew, Thomas Andrews, Harland and Wolff's thirty-nine-year-old managing director. Andrews had spent twenty-three years designing ships, and in spite of his rank he retained a common touch. Subordinates liked and re-spected him. In the words of one of those who worked for him he was "one of nature's gentlemen." Nothing escaped Andrews' attention: He oversaw everything from the design of the hull to the correct number of screws for the hat hooks in the staterooms. When Andrews learned that two Calgarians coming aboard, Albert and Vera Dick, had been married on May 31, 1911, the same day the *Titanic* had been launched, he befriended the couple.

"Bert" Dick, thirty-two, was a brash building contractor fifteen years older than his bride, Vera. He had been born in Winnipeg but was raised in Calgary when it was still a frontier town in the North West Territories. He and a brother had started a sawmill near Ponoka and by 1904 it was doing so well that Bert began selling real estate and building commercial properties in Calgary. By the time he was twenty-four he had built the Hotel Alexandra on 9th Avenue S.E., and put up the Dick Business Block on 8th Street S.E. He married Vera Gillespie in the Central Methodist Church. She was not beautiful, but in her later years she grew into a cultured, handsome woman. In 1912 she was still an awkward, socially gauche teenager. The Dicks had spent a belated honeymoon in the Holy

Land, and had returned to London to pick up solid, serviceable repro-
duction antiques for the new Tudor-style house they had built at 2111-7th
Street S. W., in Calgary's affluent Mount Royal district. The house is still
there. Their furniture had been shipped ahead on another steamer, but
there they were, two guileless tourists from Alberta being ushered aboard
the *Titanic* by one of the ship's directors. Wouldn't that be a story to share
with the folks back home? As Andrews left the couple outside the doors to
their stateroom, B-20, he shook hands with them and said, "I believe this
ship to be as nearly perfect as human brains can make her."

Bertha Mayné.
"Travelling with Quigg was a mysterious woman."
Courtesy of Herman DeWulf.

Chapter Three

If everyone who said later that they held tickets for the maiden voyage had been aboard, the *Titanic* would have turned turtle before it set sail. Contrary to the widespread impression, the ship was not filled to capacity. The seriously rich, like Harold Lovett of Ottawa, simply did not take shakedown crossings. Lovett, in fact, persuaded a family friend to cancel tickets aboard the *Titanic* precisely because it was untried. "It is foolish to take any vessel on her maiden voyage, especially one of the unprecedented dimensions of the *Titanic*," he said. "As the vessel is on trial, there is always the danger of delay on account of the engines working badly or other reasons." Still, the sailing attracted the wealthy and the titled. Lucy Noelle Martha Dyer Edwardes, otherwise known as the Countess of Rothes, was an authentic blueblood from West Tytherley, Salisbury, Wilts, going to British Columbia's Okanagan Valley to join her husband on their twelfth wedding anniversary. Her spouse, the nineteenth Earl of Rothes, was in North America looking to invest in fruit farms. The mother of two boys, one eleven the other three, she had left the children in the care of a governess, and was accompanied by her cousin, Gladys Cherry and a maid, Ruberta Maloni. The robust countess was thirty-four. She knew her position in society and made certain others respected it. To her friends, however, she wasn't the least bit stuffy. She preferred to be called Noelie because she was born at her parents London residence in Kensington on Christmas Day, loved the ocean, and was adept enough an oarswoman to navigate her own yacht on the Irish Sea.

The *Titanic's* sailing attracted an impressive list of passengers from both sides of the Atlantic: Guggenheim, Astor, Widner, and Strauss.

Elsewhere among the fashionable crowd in first class were about two

Harry Markland Molson, the richest Canadian on board,
swam away from two previous shipwrecks.
Courtesy St. Paul's Masonic Lodge No. 374, Montreal.

dozen small-time Canadian entrepreneurs like the Dicks, Baxters, and the Fortunes. The only millionaire aboard from Toronto was Major Arthur Godfrey Peuchen, a bluff, talkative commissioned officer in the Queen's Own Rifles. He had made his money in chemicals. He was president of the Standard Chemical Company, one of the first in the world to manufacture acetone (used to make explosives) from wood. Peuchen looked the part of a commanding officer. He was tall, erect, and athletic—a solid, reassuring figure. He had crossed the Atlantic at least forty times, and like all seasoned travellers, booked a cabin for comfort, not for show. His room, 104 on the C-Deck, around the corner from the Purser's Office, didn't have a porthole or private bath, but it was big enough for him and a tin box filled with $217,000 worth of stocks and bonds. Born in Montreal in 1859, Peuchen was the son of English immigrant parents. His father had been a railroad contractor in South America and his grandfather had managed the London, Brighton and Midland Railway. In 1871 Peuchen moved to Toronto where he enlisted in the Queen's Own Rifles. He was made captain in 1894, and promoted to Major ten years later. In 1911, he served as marshalling officer in charge of the Indian Cavalry at the coronation of Edward VII. He was also a lumber magnate who owned forest reserves near Hinton, Alberta. Peuchen lived with his wife Margaret, and their two children, a daughter, Jessie, sixteen, and a son, Alan, fourteen, at 599 Jarvis Street, but their real home was a country retreat on Lake Simcoe called "Woodlands," a lavish estate complete with marina, tennis courts, and a golf course. An expert yachtsman, Peuchen had been vice-commodore of the Royal St. Lawrence Yacht Club in Dorval. One of Peuchen's friends was Hugo Ross, who had crewed for him aboard his 38 tonne, 65 foot yacht *Vreda,* while he was still a student at the University of Toronto. With company refineries in England, France, and Germany, Peuchen was often away from home.

The only misgiving he had about sailing aboard the *Titanic* was about the ship's captain, Edward John Smith. Peuchen thought Smith at sixty-two much too old for the job. Self assured, amiable, and soft spoken, Smith was the perfect society captain. He spent as much time entertaining passengers as he did on the bridge. Peuchen had sailed with Smith before and was aware of the commodore's rather checkered record: Smith's first maritime mishap occurred in 1889 when he ran the *Republic* aground in New York Harbour. Two years later he ran the *Coptic* aground in Rio de Janeiro. In 1901, while he was in command of the *Majestic*, it caught fire. Damage was minimal, but Smith said afterwards he wasn't made aware of the blaze until after it had been extinguished. In 1909, he ran the *Adriatic* aground in New York and in 1911 was captain of the *Titanic's* sister ship, *Olympic* when it collided with the *Hawke*. In an interview with the *New York Times* Smith pooh-poohed the various accidents, and boasted that he had never lost a ship.

The White Star Line obviously had confidence in his abilities. After forty years at sea, taking the *Titanic* to New York on its maiden voyage was to be something of a reward before he retired. When Peuchen learned Smith was in command, he griped. "Surely we're not going to have that man."

It was Peuchen who persuaded the richest Canadian aboard, Harry Markland Molson, to extend his stay in England and sail home with him on the *Titanic*. The two were old friends. Molson was director of one of Peuchen's companies and like Peuchen was an avid yachtsman. He kept his 40 tonne, 75 foot yacht, *Alcyone* at his summer cottage in Dorval near the Royal St. Lawrence Yacht Club and served as commodore of the club in 1900-01.

Molson was a fourth-generation member of the family that had made a fortune brewing beer, banking, and building steamships. His great-great-grandfather, John Molson, came to Canada in 1782. By 1817, just ten years after Robert Fulton sent the first steamboat up the Hudson, John Molson had five steamships of his own plying the St. Lawrence River. Harry Molson was not part of the family's influential branch. He was born in 1856, and given the unusual name Markland after one of his father's business associates, G. H. Markland. He inherited his fortune in 1897 from his uncle, John Henry Robinson Molson, who left him the brewery and the bank. As president of Molson's Bank, Harry used his new found wealth to became a bon vivant, seasoned traveller, and yachtsman. *Moody's* magazine described him as "one of the most influential businessmen in Canada." His friends called him Merry Larkwand Molson. He built a house at 2 Edgehill Road in Westmount, with twelve clocks in the billiard room. He was the master of Quebec's oldest Masonic lodge, St. Paul's, #374. His photograph is still there and stands out from the crowd on the wall. It shows a sleek dandy with a broad forehead, neatly trimmed beard, and large, expressive liquid eyes. He is wearing a hounds-tooth jacket, high celluloid collar, and his lucky horseshoe diamond stickpin. Molson served as a Montreal city councillor and in 1903 was elected the first mayor of suburban Dorval. He never married and often said he was more concerned with the welfare of animals than he was with people. A major contributor to the Society for the Prevention of Cruelty to Animals, he said "people can look after themselves, animals can't." Just before he sailed to England on business he changed his will leaving his property in Dorval to his cousin's wife, Florence Morris. The codicil also gave her $30,000—more than a million in today's dollars— "to be unseizable and entirely her own property." Time has hidden the nature of their relationship, but why Molson made the last minute changes leaving a fortune to another man's wife remains intriguing. It does not, however, include any premonition of disaster. In drawing up a new will Molson was simply taking sensible precautions.

Like his friend Peuchen, he could well afford sumptuous accommodation aboard the Titanic, but he paid thirty pounds ten shillings, or about $15,000 for a relatively unpretentious inside cabin on the upper deck, C-30.

Another Montrealer travelling first class was Charles Melville Hays. He was not, as the *Montreal Star* reported, "the most notable man aboard," but he was indeed a commercial aristocrat. Born in Rock Island, Illinois, the squat, bearded railroader had moved to Canada, leaving the Wabash Railway to join the Grand Trunk Railway, which later became the Canadian National Railway. Fourteen years later, Hays was company president. Soft-spoken but stubborn, his interests other than railroading were few.

"The genius of railroading lies in patience," he once said, "in the ability to see and hear all sides of a subject then to explain why you can't do what the other fellow wants you to do."

It was Hays who convinced Prime Minister Sir Wilfrid Laurier that Canada needed a second transcontinental railroad to break the monopoly which had been created by the Canadian Pacific Railway. To this end, the Laurier government subsidized the Grand Trunk to the tune of $30 million and in November 1902, the Grand Trunk Pacific announced it would build a second transcontinental railway between Montreal and Prince Rupert, B.C. The company's majority stockholders in England were more interested in dividends than in risky expansion. Financing proved chaotic and by 1912, the Grand Trunk was $100 million in debt. Hays went to England for a directors meeting where he proposed to spend his way out of bankruptcy by upgrading rolling stock, by double tracking, and by building a chain of luxurious railway hotels across the country.

Hays, his wife Clara, and their maid, Anne Perreault were installed in suite B-69 as guests of the White Star Line's managing director, J. Bruce Ismay, who was also a director of the London North Railway. Hays was an anglophile who enjoyed hobnobbing with titled Englishmen. He kept a scrapbook of all the functions of any importance he attended, the dinner menus, and a list of all the guests.

The Hays family had spent a happy month in England. "They say I always bring sunshine to these parts and the facts appear to prove it," Hays cheerfully wrote home from London ten days before he sailed. "Clara is well and I have been feeling much better, and dyspepsia practically all gone."

While in England they had received news that the third of their four daughters, Louise, was having a difficult pregnancy and that the baby, due at the end of April, might have to be delivered by Cesarean section. Both he and his wife were anxious to get back to be with her for the birth. Hays was also coming back to Canada as head of an entourage destined for Ottawa and the gala opening on April 26 of the Grand Trunk's three million dollar flagship hotel, the Château Laurier. Hays carried with him a scratch pad of drawings for another six hostelries he planned to build: the Lord Selkirk (today the Fort Garry) in Winnipeg, the Château Qu'Appelle in Regina, the Macdonald in Edmonton, the Châteaux Miette and Mount Robson in

Clara and Charles Melville Hays were installed in suite B-69
as guests of the White Star Line's managing director.
Photo of Clara Hays courtesy of Orian Hallor.
Photo of Charles Hays courtesy of Canadian National Railways Archives.

Thornton and Orian Davidson.
Part of the Hays entourage on their way to Ottawa for the
opening of the Château Laurier Hotel.
*Photo of Thornton Davidson courtesy of the Notman Photographic
Archives of the McCord Museum of Canadian History.
Photo of Orian Davidson courtesy of Orian Hallor.*

the Canadian Rockies, and a Pacific terminus hotel in Prince Rupert.

In the adjoining cabin, B-71, was the Hays' second daughter, Orian, and her husband Thornton Davidson, the son of Charles Peers Davidson, chief justice of the Quebec Supreme Court. Davidson, thirty-two, came from an indomitable Protestant family of United Empire Loyalists. His older brother Shirley and his fiancée, Eileen Hingston drowned in Lake St. Louis in 1907 in a scandal that the family tried to cover up as a boating accident. In fact they committed suicide after Judge Davidson refused Shirley permission to marry Hingston because she was a Roman Catholic. Pleasant and unassuming, Davidson was an accomplished yachtsman, "a sailor of intrepid daring and remarkable skill." He had played hockey with the Royal Victorias, played tennis, and was good horseman. He started as a teller at the Bank of Montreal and eventually opened a brokerage house with his partner Robert Hickson. It was the Davidsons' first trip abroad.

Also travelling with the Hays family was twenty-three-year-old Vivian Payne, private secretary to Charles Hays. Payne's father, John, had worked for the Grand Trunk as an auditor, and when he died in 1903, Hays, who had no sons of his own became a surrogate father to the thirteen-year old boy.

Payne attended the High School of Montreal where he was described as "a brilliant student, his standing was won not only by his superior ability, but by hard work." After his graduation he went to work for the Grand Trunk running errands between Ottawa and Montreal. The trip with Hays was his first to England, and in a letter to his mother he was astonished at how green the countryside was in March.

Included in the Hays party was the French sculptor Paul Romain Chevré, an easily-excitable artist who divided his time between a studio at 33 Château Asinères in Paris and an office in Quebec City. The monument to Champlain in Quebec City and the statue of Marianne outside the Union Française on Viger Square in Montreal are two examples of his work. Hays had commissioned Chevré to do the marble bust of Sir Wilfrid Laurier for the hotel lobby, and he was to be present for its unveiling.

Chevré was a seasoned traveller who had shuffled across the Atlantic twice a year for fourteen years. He would spend six months in Canada obtaining commissions and the other six months in France where he would execute the sculptures. In spite of his many trips he had the same apprehension about getting on a ship that some people today have about sitting on an airplane. His stateroom, A-7, was on the Upper Promenade Deck conveniently located a few steps from the Reading and Writing room, where Chevré could work on his designs, and not far from the Gentlemen's Smoking Room, where he could indulge his passion for poker. The outside cabin, ahead of the first funnel, was considered one of the safest locations on the ship, directly below the life boats.

"Hud" Allison another young, self-made millionaire on board, was a stock promoter who divided his time between his office in Montreal and a stock farm near Chesterville, Ontario, just south of Ottawa where he and his brother raised Clydesdales, Hackneys, and Holsteins. Allison was the junior partner in the Montreal firm of Johnson, McConnell, and Allison, and was reputed to be worth "between one and two million dollars."

Hudson Joshua Allison was born on the family farm on December 9, 1881, and as a teenager worked behind the counter of the local general store. Slender and saturnine, with a good head for figures, he was imbued with the Protestant work ethic. When he was nineteen his uncle, Frank Johnson, hired the bespectacled youth to head the junior division of the brokerage firm he had started with John Wilson McConnell, who would later buy the *Montreal Star*. The three men were members of Montreal's so-called "Methodist Mafia," upstarts in Canadian financial circles. Allison was sent to Buffalo to learn shorthand, worked as an insurance agent for his uncle at Sun Life and New York Life, then went to Winnipeg, where he opened an office. During his two years there "he resided at the corner of Westminster Avenue and Sherbrooke Street in the upper part of George Markle's house."

During one of his frequent train trips back east he met Bess Waldo Daniels, the young but matronly daughter of an Irish-American Milwaukee factory clerk. They were married against her parents' wishes in Milwaukee, Wisconsin, on his twenty-sixth birthday in 1907. She had just turned twenty-one. They were a pious couple, described by one relative as "very churchy people." Militant evangelism was a constant presence in their lives. Allison's business correspondence on file in the McConnell papers at the McGill Archives is filled with fleeting references to their church work, teaching Sunday School, Bible classes ,and even his filling in as lay preacher from time to time. Their daughter, Helen Loraine, was born on June 5, 1909, and their son, Trevor two years later, on May 7, 1911. The same year Allison began the Allison Stock Farm, and built a new house on the farm and another in Westmount. He was on the board of directors of the British Canadian Lumber Corporation and he and his wife and children sailed to London for a working vacation. During the six-week trip they had Trevor baptized at Epworth in a church where the founder of their religion, John Wesley had preached. They took a side trip to the Scottish Highlands where they bought two dozen Clydesdale and Hackney stallions and mares for the farm. At the same time, they picked up furniture for their houses, and recruited four new servants in London: two English nannies for the children, Alice Cleaver and Sarah Daniels; a cook, Mildrid Brown, and a chauffeur, George Swane. The nurse they had originally hired to look after Trevor decided at the last minute not to take the job, and Alice Cleaver was hastily engaged as a replacement. Three years earlier, Cleaver had been convicted of throwing her ten-week-old son Reggie, who had been born out of wedlock, from a moving train. She was sentenced to be hanged but the sentence was commuted and Cleaver was released after six months in prison. It is highly unlikely the Allisons were aware of Alice Cleaver's murderous past when they hired her, although at least one family member believes they did. A cousin suggested that the Allisons took pity on Cleaver, and hired her out of a sense of Christian duty so that she might be rehabilitated and start a new life in a new country.

Like many others on the *Titanic*, the Allisons had altered their original travel plans to be among the wealthy and prominent on a maiden voyage. They paid 151 pounds for two lavish staterooms on Upper Deck, C22-26, that cost the equivalent of $75,000.

Returning to his home in Halifax was the natty entrepreneur and realtor

George Wright, who had made his fortune publishing *Wright's World Business Directories*. Wright was born a farmer's son in Tufts Cove, Nova Scotia, in 1849. In 1876, during a visit to the U.S. centennial exhibition in Philadelphia, he got the idea of printing an international business directory, and became a successful printer before he was thirty. His directories were an indispensable guide to the corporate world on three continents. The sixty-two-year-old bachelor with a handsome handlebar mustache was a well-travelled but private individual who tended to let his hair down only when with friends. A member of the Bachelor's Club he enjoyed hunting, fishing, and dancing, and he owned two yachts, *The Princess* and *Alba*. He was a philanthropist and something of a prude. When David Belasco's play *The Girl of the Golden West* opened, Wright objected to the language and pronounced it immoral. When movies came to Halifax, Wright complained that *Little Red Riding Hood* and *Visit to the Mother-in-Law* were unfit as family entertainment. He also led a campaign against obscenity, gambling, and anything that he considered to be indecent literature. He was, however, also a prominent construction contractor who built a number of houses and public buildings on Barrington Street, including the Marble-Wright building, at number 1672 and the Saint Paul building, at 1684 which still stand, as does his house at 989 Young Ave. He was committed to better housing for the working poor, and he created a subdivision along South Park in Halifax which was remarkable for the time because it was one of the first to integrate houses for the rich and the poor. Wright had been in Paris when he learned of the *Titanic's* maiden voyage, and decided to sail home aboard the ship. Suspicious of strangers, he declined to have his name included on the printed list of ship's passengers distributed during the voyage. Although we know he paid twenty-six pounds for his ticket, there is no record of which cabin he was assigned, but it was a single berth cabin, probably on E Deck where many of the commercial travellers like George Edward Graham, a buyer with the T. Eaton Company in Winnipeg, were booked.

Graham was one of several salesmen travelling first class, and appears to have been in an upgraded cabin, C-42. Born on a farm near St. Mary's,

George Wright.
He slept through the whole disaster.
Public Archives of Nova Scotia, N-6323.

T. Eaton Co. buyer George Graham (top row, second
from left) and his brothers. His last cable to his
wife said he was well.
St. Mary's Museum.

Ontario, in 1873, the sixth of seven brothers, he went to work at seventeen as a hardware clerk in St. Mary's, worked for awhile in Galt, then moved to Toronto where he got a job with Eaton's department store. A genial, dark good-looking man with a jaunty demeanour, he worked his way through the ranks. He married Edith May Jackson from Harriston, Ontario, in 1905, and they were active in the Methodist church—two of Graham's brothers were ministers. When Eaton's opened its store in Winnipeg in 1906, Graham was transferred to Manitoba to head its crockery and fine china division. The move was said to be traumatic for his wife, who was unhappy to leave her family and friends behind. Their son, John Humphrey, was born in August 1908 but died in January 1911. Shortly after his death, Edith suffered a miscarriage. She remained despondent and never recovered fully from the loss. Graham was reluctant to leave his wife by herself in Winnipeg, but his job required him to go to England, Belgium, and Austria on an annual spring buying trip. He made arrangements for her to stay with her parents in Harriston while he was away and for her to meet him in Toronto when he returned. He was originally scheduled to sail on the *Mauretania,* but when he discovered he could get home to his wife three days sooner if he took the *Titanic,* he changed his travel plans.

Also bound for Toronto was John James Borebank, who divided his time between a home in West Hallam, Derbyshire, and a realty office in Canada. He was born in West Hallam in 1870 and emigrated to Canada as a youngster with his parents who opened a grocery store in Toronto. Borebank moved to Winnipeg in 1896, and after establishing a business there, returned to Toronto where he opened an office in the Quebec Bank building on King Street. He enrolled his daughter, Eileen, in a school in England, and in 1911 took an extended vacation which allowed him and his wife, Isabel, to spend time with her, and to attend the coronation of George V. They had planned to stay in England until September, but Borebank was unexpectedly called to Toronto to deal with a management crisis.

Stockbroker Austen Partner from Tolworth, Surbiton, England, was going first to Toronto then Winnipeg. The father of two boys, one nine, the other twelve, Partner was on his seventeenth trip to Canada. He had started a new job with the firm of Myer and Robertson ten days earlier, and he was going to Canada to familiarize himself with the offices of an affiliated firm, Robinson and Black. Partner was in E-58.

A few doors away in E-63 was Edward Pomery Colley, a surveyor who worked for prominent British Columbia industrialist James Dunsmuir. Colley was heading for Victoria on Vancouver Island after a vacation in his native Ireland, and would turn thirty-seven on April 15. Little else is known about him, but one fellow passenger described him as "a roly-poly Irishman who laughed a lot but said little."

What is astonishing about most of the Canadians travelling first class is not only how rich they were, but how young. Vera Dick was seventeen; Charles Fortune, nineteen, his sisters all in their early twenties. So were Quigg Baxter and his sister Zette. Hudson Allison was thirty; his wife Bessie, only twenty-four, Vivian Payne was twenty-three. They all came aboard in a bustle of lighthearted activity and to one reporter it seemed like one big reunion of expatriates. "No one had to consult the passenger list," he wrote, "They met as one big party."

Chapter Four

FIRST CLASS PASSENGERS assumed a proprietary air of the ship and didn't mingle with, or care to know anyone else on board. They were, of course, prepared to share the liner with the socially inferior in second class and steerage so long as those second and third class passengers remained out of sight. There was nothing shabby, however, about second class accommodation aboard the *Titanic*. The quarters were as good as those in first class on almost any other ship at the time. Staterooms lined corridors carpeted in two shades of either green or burgundy and were decorated in a basic off-white. Cabins were small but they contained comfortable sleeping berths, an upholstered couch, a mahogany wash stand with polished brass fittings. Cut glass light fixtures illuminated the rooms. The second class promenade was located aft, around the ship's decorative fourth funnel. The staircase reserved for second class passengers led to an oak-panelled smoking room on B deck; it boasted beamed ceilings, leaded glass windows, and plush chairs. There was a library with books housed in glass cases on C Deck and a well-appointed dining salon on D Deck.

Leopold Weisz was travelling second class but he was a walking gold mine. Literally. The thirty-three-year-old Hungarian-born Jewish stone carver had sewn $30,000 in currency, his life savings, into the lining of his suit. In addition, he had $15,000 in gold bullion stashed in his pockets. Weisz, a worldly Magyar, grew up in the Elizabeth district of Pest, and when he was nineteen went to England to study at the Bromsgrove Guild of Applied Art. In 1911, he found work in Montreal carving the frieze for the Museum of Fine Arts building on Sherbrooke Street, then was contracted to do the stone shields which decorate the Dominion Express building at the corner of St. Jacques Street West and St. François Xavier. Montreal was in the midst of a building boom, and so many other commissions followed he decided "Quebec was the place to make money from art." He went into partnership with a building contractor, Edward Lancelot Wren, and went back to England to fetch his wife, Mathilde Françoise Pede. The couple were to have sailed first class on another ship, but because of the coal strike, they were transferred to the *Titanic*.

Also on his way to Montreal was a thirty-five-year-old rubber merchant from Liverpool, Joseph J. Fynney, going to visit his widowed seventy-one-year-old mother, Frances. Fynney's father had died in 1894, and shortly afterwards his mother moved to Montreal to live with her daughter, Martha Hoseason. Fynney's neighbours recall that he was a man of "exceptional good looks, but a bit of a Nancy boy." Fynney worked with delinquent youngsters at his parish church, St. James, Toxeth, and local gossip had it that his interest in some of his charges was more than spiritual. Rumours circulated about his conduct with some of the young men who rang his doorbell at 13 Parkway at all hours of the night. He often travelled to Canada to visit his mother, and each time he made the trip it was in the company of a male teenager. On this occasion, his travelling companion was Alfred Gaskell, a swarthy seventeen-year old apprentice barrel maker with youthful looks and an attractive open face.

René-Jacques Levy, a thirty-six-year-old chemist from Paris, was also bound for Montreal. He had emigrated to Quebec with his wife and three daughters in 1910, and had returned to France for a family funeral. He was originally scheduled to sail on the *France*, but changed his reservations when he learned the *Titanic* would get him home ten days earlier.

Most of the passengers in second class were upper middle-class professionals, people like Dr. Alfred Pain who was going home to Hamilton, Ontario, after a year of post-graduate studies at Kings College Hospital in London. Tall, earnest, and vulnerable, Pain was only twenty-four, one of the youngest surgeons ever to graduate from the University of Toronto's medical school. The son of a Hamilton greengrocer, he was an accomplished musician who played both flute and piano. He was also an expert marksman, and a yachtsman. He had hoped to sign on as a ship doctor on

Hamilton's Alfred Pain was one of the youngest surgeons
ever to granduate from the University of Toronto's
medical school.
University of Toronto Archives.

Hilda Slayter, the genteel, cultivated daughter of a Halifax
doctor, was on her way to British Columbia to be married.
Courtesy of Beatrice Lacon.

a freighter in exchange for free passage home. When that didn't materialize, he bought a ticket on a tramp steamer that was supposed to be sailing to New York. There were last minute changes to its destination, and Pain switched to the *Titanic*. He was travelling as a social escort with Margaret Wright, an English friend who was coming to America to marry her childhood sweetheart, Arthur Woolcott, who had gone to Cottage Grove, Oregon, where he had started farming. With them was Norman Douglas, a young Scottish engineer from Glasgow on his way to Vancouver.

Frank Maybery, a thirty-seven-year old realtor, was leaving his wife and children behind in Weston-Super-Mare, a small seaside town on England's west coast to return to Moose Jaw, Saskatchewan, to help run his older brother's business. His brother Alfred first discovered Moose Jaw when he was in Canada, returning to England from the Orient in 1904. He was impressed with the potential of the place. Sniffing an opportunity to make money in what was about to become a new Canadian province, Alfred persuaded Frank to join him in Canada. When the two brothers went into the real estate business in the spring of 1906, Moose Jaw was booming. There were over 113 listed real estate agencies, even though the city only had a population of 15,000. Their office in the Dominion Bank building at 40 Main Street, specialized in selling farmland, much of it around the Mortlach area. Maybery is remembered as being pinched and aloof. A more charitable description suggests he was "a man of very careful thought, definite and clear, a man of faith whose religious experience was not always on his lips." He was active in St. Andrews' Presbyterian Church and was a founding member of the YMCA in Moose Jaw. The Maybery brothers were successful land speculators. Frank's wife, Ella, who considered herself an aristocrat among the rowdy, grew homesick for Somerset. In the autumn of 1911, Maybery took her and their two young daughters, Ruth and Nancy, back to England. In January 1912, Alfred was elected mayor of Moose Jaw and asked Frank to return to look after their business while he tended to civic duties. Maybery was travelling aboard the *Titanic* with a family friend, the Rev. Charles Kirkland, a sturdy Scots Presbyterian minister who was going to to visit a sister in Tuxford, Saskatchewan.

Hilda Slayter, the genteel cultivated daughter of a Halifax doctor, was on her way to British Columbia to be married. Her fiancé, Harry Reginald Dunbar Lacon, lived on Denman Island. Slayter had left home in 1902 to study music in Italy. She had hoped to become a professional singer. Her older brother had been an officer aboard the *Victoria and Albert*, Queen Victoria's yacht, and helped support her. Her voice was pleasant enough but her ambition exceeded her talent. By the time she was twenty-seven she was unmarried and realized her career was going nowhere. That is when she met Harry Lacon, the son of British M.P. and baron, Sir Edmund Henry Knowles Lacon of Ottley. Harry had been sent down from Eton and was banished to Canada. He persuaded her that she was the girl for him. According to a member of the family Harry was a remittance man, but there wasn't much remittance. He was a mess. The only thing in his favour was that he was unmarried. He was her last chance. Hilda had spent two months in England shopping for her trousseau. In her trunks were "one satin opal and pearl wedding dress, with silver opal and mesh scarf, satin slippers, silk stockings, and hair bandeau," which she claimed cost $4,000. As well, there was a "blue satin silver net dress, silver and blue scarf, silver tissue and osprey, and Italian embroidered lace hand made blouses," worth another $3,000.

Benjamin Hart, a building contractor from Ilford, Essex, just outside London, was emigrating to Canada with his wife Esther and their seven-year-old daughter Eva. They were bound for Winnipeg where Hart was going to open a hardware store. Hart had a friend in Canada who had done remarkably well and it was he who had persuaded the Harts to join him. "It was all decided in the space of an evening," said his daughter. The Harts had booked passage to Canada on another ship, but because of the coal strike they were transferred to the *Titanic*. "From that moment my mother was smitten with a terrible premonition of disaster," Eva remembered. "She knew there was something terribly wrong. When she saw a headline in a newspaper that their new ship was unsinkable she said, 'Now I know why I am frightened. This is flying in the face of God.' And that really hit me as a seven year old. You can imagine a child suddenly being told that someone

"Smitten with a premonition of disaster."
Benjamin and Esther Hart with daughter Eva.

is flying in the face of God." So even before they boarded, Mrs. Hart and her daughter were apprehensive. "From the time we went aboard that ship my mother never went to bed at night. She sat up all night and slept peacefully through the day."

Pioneer filmmaker, William H. Harbeck, was on his way to Montreal to make a film for the Canadian Pacific Railway. Harbeck hailed from Toledo, Ohio, where his wife lived, but he spent so much of his time working in Canada that everyone thought of him as a native. He earned his reputation for his film of the aftermath of the 1906 San Francisco earthquake, before the Canadian Pacific Railway's department of colonization hired him in 1910 "to put Western Canada on the motion picture screen in a scenic, industrial and comic form." Harbeck turned out thirteen one-reelers, promotional shorts that were designed to attract European immigrants to Canada. Movies were just coming into their own in 1912. North America's first movie theatre, the Ouimetoscope in Montreal was only six years old. Cultivated adults regarded movies with disdain but uneducated city dwellers were taken with the new medium. Harbeck 's films had been so successful the CPR had hired him to do a feature on Alaska and had sent him to Paris to study with Leon Gaumont, the trailblazing French filmmaker who first mastered the location shoot, a feature that continues to mark French cinema. One of Harbeck's first features, *The Ship's Husband*, was a light comedy about a complicated matrimonial mix-up on a boat running between Vancouver and Victoria. Harbeck was involved in his own real-life matrimonial complexities. Although he was a married man with two teen-age boys, the woman he had registered with him as his wife, wasn't. She was Henriette Yrois, a twenty-four-year-old model Harbeck had met in Paris.

James Matthew McCrie of Sarnia, Ontario, had been in Arabia working on an oil drilling rig when he learned that one of his three children had been diagnosed with tuberculosis, and was not expected to live. He was on his way home to comfort his distraught wife.

Ernest Sjöstedt, an eminent mining engineer and metallurgist, was also returning from the Middle East to visit his wife in Canada. Sjöstedt, originally from Hjo, Sweden, apprenticed at the Creusot Iron Works in

France then emigrated to the United States in 1878. He worked for Bethlehem Steel in Pennsylvania and in 1890 moved to Canada to work for the Nova Scotia Steel Company in Bridgeville. There he met and married Jesse Kathleen Winslow, and they had two daughters. He was then hired by the Lake Superior Steel company and moved to Sault Ste. Marie, Ontario. He was the inventor of the Sjöstedt Sulphur Roaster, and the Sjöstedt Electric Smelting Furnace. He had been abroad studying German innovations in smelting.

About five hundred third class passengers embarked at Southampton, most of them British and Scandinavian. Nineteen-year-old George Sage, the eldest son in a family of nine, was going to Saskatchewan to strike out on his own. A year earlier he and his father, John, had left their home in Peterborough to see what opportunities Canada had to offer. They worked as cooks for the Canadian Pacific Railway during the summer of 1911 and spent some time looking for farm land in Saskatchewan. In the end, John Sage decided to uproot his family and move to Florida instead. But George, who had fallen in love with a young woman in western Canada decided to go back to the midwest and pursue the romance. He was travelling with his mother, Annie, and his brothers and sisters, Thomas, Constance, Ada, William, Dorothy, Frederick, Douglas, and Stella, who ranged in age from three to twenty-two. Annie Sage left England heartsick, longing for what she had left behind and afraid of where she was going. A superstitious woman, she had been apprehensive about the voyage across the Atlantic because her fourteen-year-old daughter, Dorothy, had once fallen into a well and had been saved from drowning. Annie believed an old wive's tale which taught that death by drowning could not be cheated, and that a person rescued from water would eventually die in water.

Shortly before leaving their home in Peterborough, Annie entrusted an album of family photographs to a friend. "I won't be needing this where I am going," she said tearfully. "I don't want my precious pictures to be food for the fishes." Stella Sage was not nearly as pessimistic. Her parents had told her that if she did not like life in America they would pay her return fare to England. She already had made up her mind. In a postcard she dashed off to a friend back home, she wrote, "I am not seasick yet, and hope I shall not be ... Will write a long letter while on the boat. Cheer up, I'm coming back soon."

The Braund bothers, twenty-nine-year-old Lewis Richard, and twenty-two-year-old Owen Harris, set out with raw hope from Devonshire to settle in the Qu'Appelle Valley in Saskatchewan. Then there were the Hickman brothers, Lewis, Leonard, and Stanley, from Fritham, on their way to The Pas, Manitoba. Lewis, thirty-two, the eldest, had already spent six years in northern Manitoba, and so enthralled the family with stories of his life on the Canadian frontier that his two younger siblings decided to join him.

John Garfith, a twenty-one-year-old shoemaker from Wollaston, near Wellington, England, was one of a family of nine. His mother was widowed and he had hoped to be able to support her by obtaining work in Canada. His lifelong friend and neighbour, George Patchett, also twenty-one, had a brother who had emigrated to Berlin (today Kitchner), Ontario and who had done well for himself. Garfith and Patchett decided to follow. Both were booked to sail out of Liverpool aboard the *Empress of Britain,* but their train was late. They missed the ship, but managed to exchange their tickets for passage on the *Titanic.*

Harold Reynolds, a twenty-one-year-old baker from 10 Courthill Road, in London, was on his way to join a friend in Toronto.

The voyage was a fantasy for nine-year-old Ingeborg Constancia Andersson and her eleven-year-old sister, Sigrid Elizabeth. The two daughters of Andrew John Andersson, thirty-nine, and his wife, Alfrida Konstantina, shared the same birthday, April 16, and were looking forward to celebrating at sea. The Andersson family, including three other children, Ebba Iris Alfrida, seven, Ellis Anna Maria, two, and three-year-old Sigvard Harald Elias, were leaving Kisa, Sweden, to begin a new life in Winnipeg. They had been persuaded to emigrate to Canada by Mrs. Andersson's sister, Mrs. Sigrid Danbom, and her husband, Ernest, who had bought a farm in Stanton, Iowa. The Danboms were accompanying the Anderssons and were going to stop in Winnipeg to visit relatives before continuing to their homestead in the United States.

Karl Johan Wiklund, twenty-one, and his younger brother Jacob Alfred Wiklund, eighteen, had been farm hands in their native Finland. They were emigrating to Quebec's Eastern Townships. Other Finns emigrating to Canada included Isak Nirva and his wive Maija Lisa, as well as Nokolai Kallio, Matti Maenpaad, and Matti Rintamaki, all going to Sudbury, Ontario.

At noon on April 10, all passengers were at last aboard, and the ship's second officer, Charles Lightoller, remarked "that from end to end, the *Titanic* which had for several days been like a nest of bees now resembled a hive about to swarm."

With a throaty blast from her horns, the *Titanic* slipped her moorings. Passengers threw flowers from the deck as it set sail. Rowland Southell, who saw the ship leave, remembered all the people on deck were waving and throwing flowers down. "They were all going into the sea." Marconi's daughter, Degna, was there to wave goodbye to the *Titanic*, "huge and resplendent in the spring sunlight, and dozens of handkerchiefs and scarves waved back at us." As the *Titanic* pulled away there was a thrilling but unnerving incident as some people aboard imagined they heard gunshots being fired. It wasn't gunfire, but the sound of mooring lines being snapped. Suction caused by the *Titanic's* displacement of water pulled the smaller *New York* into the *Titanic's* path. Until the *Titanic* reversed engines, a collision between the two ships seemed inevitable. Filmmaker Harbeck turned his cameras on the *New York* and "followed the whole scene with eager eyes, turning the handle of his camera with most evident pleasure as he recorded the unexpected incident on his films." One eyewitness called it "a narrow squeak for all of us." The commotion died down and the *Titanic* headed out past the Isle of Wight into the English Channel to pick up passengers in the French seaport, Cherbourg. It arrived one hour behind schedule.

Neshan Krekorian, Brantford, Ontario, July 1912.
"Cooped up in steerage like a chicken."
Courtesy of Alice Solomonian.

Chapter Five

A TRAVEL AGENT in Marseilles took advantage of Neshan Krekorian, a Christian Armenian who was determined to go to Canada. He and five compatriots—Sarkis Mardirosian, Orsen Sirayanian, Ortin Zakarian, Maprieder Zarkarian, and David Vartunian, all from the village of Keghi in what was then Turkish-occupied Armenia, had decided to flee their country and emigrate to Brantford, Ontario, after Turkish Muslims renewed an ongoing vendetta against Christians. Unlike the others, Krekorian did not have a ticket. He dickered with a passenger agent in Marseilles and later said he had to pay a bribe to get aboard with his companions. Born in Turkey on May 12, 1886, Krekorian was a strong young man—muscular, illiterate but intelligent. He was not especially happy to be travelling in a new boat, "cooped up like a chicken" in steerage. Unlike Krekorian, the lives of most of those steerage passengers are as impenetrable as the depths of the ocean they attempted to cross. A microcosm of Central Europe and the Middle East, emigrants aboard the *Titanic* outnumbered first class passengers two to one. At least a dozen of them were Syrians going to Ottawa.

It is difficult to determine exactly who they were. The spelling of their names on the passenger list varies. To confuse matters, some had their names anglicized before sailing and often the same person was listed under several variations of the same name. In other instances, first names were listed as family names. Some may have been left off the passenger list altogether. One passenger for certain was Mariana Assaf, a forty-five-year-old Ottawa resident who had returned to Syria to visit the two teenage sons she had left behind in the village of Kfar Mechki when she first came to Canada. With her was a young cousin, Gerious Assaf, and her nephew,

69

twenty-seven-year-old Solomon Khalil. Khalil had gone back to find a bride. Joseph Caram, a merchant who had a shop at 205 Broad Street in Ottawa, had also gone back to Syria to get married and was returning to Canada with his eighteen-year-old bride, Maria Elias. With them was her father Joseph Elias and her seventeen-year-old brother, Tannous. Katherine David Barbara and her daughter Soude were returning with the party as well.

There were also two naturalized Canadian journalists, Mansour Hanna and Mansour Novel who lived in Ottawa but who had left their families behind in Syria. Heading for Mahone Bay, Nova Scotia were twelve-year-old Elias and fourteen-year-old Jemila Nicola-Yarred from Hakour, a small mountain village north of Beirut. The voyage was fraught with anxiety even before it began. Their father failed the medical because of an eye infection and was not permitted aboard. So he sent his children ahead with a party of eleven relatives.

From Turkish Lebanon came Sultani Boulos, and her two children, Akar and Nourelain, aged nine and seven, who were going to join her husband in Kent county, Ontario.

Like all ships, the *Titanic* transported every sort of emigrant: dreamers, the industrious, misfits, and failures. Even in their Sunday best no one would ever mistake a passenger in third class for anything else. They gave themselves away by the pallor of their skin, their clothing, and by the way they moved. They looked older, younger. No matter how decent or how hardworking most of them were, they were perceived as being so inconsequential that few took note of them. Yet it was the emigrant fares that kept the ships afloat. In the twelve years since the Canadian government had opened the country to wholesale immigration, 1.75 million arrived, boosting the country's population by 40 percent. Everyone else aboard the ship looked down on emigrants as a scruffy lot of inferior ethnic and moral stock. The prevailing attitude was summed up by one travel writer in the 1912 guidebook, *Travelling Palaces:* "Most British liners will not carry emigrants from Central Europe because of their dirty habits. This may seem unkind, but if you were to see the disgusting conditions of some of the men and women who come from that part of the continent, you would not wonder at the restrictions but would be surprised that they were allowed to enter a railway train—even a fourth class Continental."

Third class accommodation was spartan but functional. Married passengers were confined to quarters in the bow and in the stern on F and G decks. There were dormitories for the men, as well as tiny pine-panelled cabins that could sleep two, six, eight, or ten. There were also portable rooms, enclosed by steel partitions that could be moved at will to create whatever space was required to accommodate those who were sailing. The only way those housed in front of the ship could get to those in the rear, however, was by a vast corridor known as Scotland Road that ran almost the entire length of the ship on E Deck.

Phillipe Wiseman, a coarse jack-of-all-trades who had squandered what little money he had on a binge in Europe, was returning to Quebec City. A fifty-four-year-old father of seven, Wiseman had worked as stevedore, lumberjack, and farmhand. Although he was separated from his wife, he owned a house just across the street from where she lived in Quebec City's lower town. There was also Leo Zimmerman, twenty-nine, a Swiss national, about whom little is known except that he was travelling to Montreal.

Two hundred and seventy-five passengers boarded the *Titanic* at Cherbourg. There were thirty second class passengers, among whom were Albert Mallet, a cognac importer with the Montreal liquor firm, Laporte, Martin and Co., his wife, Antoinette, and their three-year-old son, André. They were returning to their home in Montreal after visiting relatives in France. The Mallets had planned to return on a French ship, but like many others "sold the tickets they had procured to take passage on the *Titanic*." Travelling with the Mallets was a family friend, twenty-three-year-old Émile Richard. Richard had just finished his compulsory tour of duty in the French army and his father was sending him on a Canadian vacation before he went to work at the family distillery.

The *Titanic* left Cherbourg as the sun faded into streaks of brilliant orange, indigo, and red. Sea dogs recalled the ancient mariner's ditty, "red sky at night, sailor's delight," and anticipated a smooth, uneventful crossing. Before the ship began its run across the Atlantic, there was one more stop.

Titanic arrived at Cobh, today known as Queenstown, at 11:30 Thursday morning and tenders ferried another 120 passengers on board, all but seven of them in steerage. There were perhaps as many as a dozen heading for Canada, including twenty-four-year-old Patrick Colbert, who was leaving Kilconlea, Abbeyfeale, to join his brother, Christopher, as a monk in a monastery at St. Patrick's Academy in Sherbrooke, Quebec. Colbert, a serious, mannered man, had worked as a porter at the local railway station where he was cited for his "industry, intelligence and tem-perate habits." Brigit O'Sullivan was coming to Canada from County Cork because her brother in Montreal had convinced her that the city offered "a better oppor-tunity for young women." Thomas Rowan Morrow, thirty-one, realizing the ambition of a lifetime, packed his earthly possessions in a pasteboard suitcase and dreamed of making his fortune in Alberta. He was leaving County Down to join his brother, Waddell, on a ranch near Gleichen. Morrow was an Orangeman, and local Worshipful Master of his Masonic lodge in Rathfriland. He was probably taking advantage of subsidized fares to Canada offered by the British government to shorten relief rolls in Britain. Seventy percent of those who took advantage of the government program and came to Canada were eventually deported back to Britain as undesirables.

The best that can be said about steerage is that the beds were clean and the food was wholesome. The passengers were virtually confined to their quarters in the bowels of the ship. United States immigration law required those in third class to be separated from first and second class passengers to prevent the spread of infectious disease. So, as the *Titanic* left Cobh, passengers stood on deck and watched as the great gothic walls of St. Coleman's Cathedral high on a hill above the seaport, dropped below the horizon. A piper played *Erin's Lament,* and as the *Titanic* left the coast of Ireland behind, the stairwells and exits leading up from the lowest decks were securely locked. Steerage passengers would be quarantined for the duration of the voyage. The ship could carry 3,000, but it was not booked to capacity as it headed out to sea. Tickets had been issued to 1,316 passengers, and with its crew of 892, it carried 2,208.

"If," said one contemporary,

> thinking of the *Titanic* you could imagine her to be split in half
> from bow to stern so that you could look, as one looks at the
> section of a hive, upon all her manifold life thus suddenly laid bare,
> you would find in her a microcosm of civilized society. Up on top
> are the rulers, surrounded by the rich and the luxurious, enjoying
> the best of everything; a little way below them, their servants and
> parasites, ministering not so much to their necessities as to their
> luxuries; lower down still, at the base and foundation of all, the
> fierce and terrible labour of the stoke holds where the black slaves
> are shovelling as though for dear life, endlessly pouring coal into
> furnaces that devoured it and yet ever demanded a new supply—
> horrible labour, joyless life and yet the labour that gives life and
> movement to the whole ship. Up above are the beautiful things,
> the pleasant things. Up above are the people who rest and enjoy;
> down below the people who sweat and suffer.

Montreal's Baxter family paid £247 to occupy these staterooms,
B58-60, the *Titanic*'s second-most expensive suites.
Courtesy of Harland and Wolff.

Chapter Six

ON EVERY TRANSATLANTIC voyage there is a moment when time seems suspended and passengers are lulled into lethargy by the motion of the grey Atlantic swells, pregnant and powerful. There is something enthralling about being so remote. Adding to the calm aboard the *Titanic* were the mix of fresh scents that accompany a maiden voyage: varnish and wax and paint, the smell of leather steamer trunks, the stinging whiff of cinders and brine. On the first day out the sea was smooth. Passengers took time to explore the ship and to orient themselves. The geographical point of reference for first class passengers was the magnificent grand staircase between the first and second funnels, a mix of seventeenth century English-style William and Mary design with French Louis XIV balustrades. Topped by a huge Art Nouveau frosted glass dome, the staircase was almost an atrium which provided graceful access to all the amenities the ship had to offer on six decks. Second class passengers discovered they had an electric escalator of their own. Third class passengers took to their General Room, plainly fitted out in white enamel, or strolled their own promenade on the Shelter Deck. The ship was so large it took Second Officer Charles Lightoller two weeks to find his way with confidence from one end of it to the other. Lightoller was no neophyte. Nicknamed Lucky Lights because he had survived five shipwrecks, he was, at thirty-eight, an adventurer, a world traveller who had set out for the Klondike to pan for gold when he was twenty-four.

By late afternoon on the first day out, many of the women took advantage of the good weather to swan around the decks in their kimono wraps, read or write letters, or just lounge on their deck chairs and watch the endlessly changing ocean. One passenger, Arthur Gee, a textile merchant on his way from Russia to Mexico, wrote to a relative in Kuroki,

Saskatchewan. "I have never seen anything so magnificent, even in a first class hotel. I might be living in a palace. We seem to be miles above the water and there are certainly miles of promenade deck. The lobbies are so long that they appear to come to a point in the distance. Just finished dinner. They call us up to dress by bugle. It reminded me of some Russian villages where they call the cattle home from the fields."

There was a certain protocol that had to be observed. Much of the time shipboard was spent dressing for breakfast, lunch, and dinner. First class passengers required a change of clothes at least four times daily. Leisurely afternoons drifted into languid evenings. The most demanding decision any of the pampered first class passengers had to make was what wine to drink with dinner. There was no formal program of ship board activities. Passengers amused themselves. French-speaking passengers like Paul Chevré and Quigg Baxter gravitated to the bright and airy Café Parisien on B Deck, an imitation sidewalk café where the waiters spoke French, pastis was on the menu and the coffee was strong. In the reception room outside the café you could hear a trio—a violinist, cellist, and pianist.

Hugo Ross was ill in bed, but not without a steady parade of visitors to cheer him up. The Fortune sisters, Major Peuchen, Thomas McCaffry, and Thomson Beattie took turns visiting him. Hélène Baxter became seasick and barely ventured out of her stateroom. That made it easier for Quigg to slip away for his romantic interludes with Berthe Mayné. Charles Fortune and Thornton Davidson worked out in the gym and squash court. To keep in shape they pedalled the stationary bicycle or boxed with a punching bag. The more energetic passengers used the swimming pool on F Deck or indulged themselves in the Turkish baths.

One of the ship's young stewards, a man by the name of Jones, not much older than Vera Dick, became infatuated with her. Much to her husband's annoyance, Vera encouraged his attention.

In second class, filmmaker William Harbeck watched his "wife" Henrietta Yrois play solitaire for hours on end and occasionally kibitzed over her shoulder. Young Alfred Gaskell buried his head in the goose down pillows and revelled in it all.

Those in a gambling mood could enter the pool on the ship's run, and wager on how many nautical miles it covered each day. Each day at noon the distance the ship had travelled the previous day was posted: Thursday, 386; Friday, 519; and Saturday, 546.

Everyone crossing the North Atlantic was well aware of the ice hazard and fully expected to see bergs, growlers, bergies, pack-ice, and ice pans during the voyage. Icebergs are calved from glaciers in the fjords of Northern Labrador and the western coast Greenland, and each spring make their way into the Gulf Stream. Some are lethal, floating islands towering 200 feet above the surface of the water with 90 percent of their mass underneath. Unlike sea ice, icebergs are not, as many believe, frozen water but sheets of hard-packed, compressed snow that is piled up for centuries. The increasing weight causes the ice sheets to move and slide from their rocky underpinnings until they slip towards the sea where they float away, jagged peaks in huge numbers. They are impossible to chart with accuracy. Ships can record where they are when they are spotted; they cannot tell what their position will be in an hour. The Nova Scotia and Bay of Fundy Pilot and the Hydrographic Office at the Admiralty both spelled out the safest route ships should follow to avoid "extensive fields of solid compact ice."

"Ice is more likely to be encountered in this route between April and August, although icebergs have been seen at all seasons north of the 43rd parallel," they warned. "It would appear that while the southernmost limits are at about 42°N and 45° W, icebergs may be met with much farther south from Newfoundland, in April, May, and June. They have been seen as far as 39°N. It is impossible to give any distinct idea where ice may be expected. Everything must depend on the vigilance, caution, and skill with which a vessel is navigated."

The *Titanic* reached the northern waters off the coast of Newfoundland. Streaks of dawn washed the silent sea with burnt orange on the morning of April 14. It encountered a number of ships heading west including the *Caronia, Baltic, Amerika*, and *Mesaba*. Each in turn warned the *Titanic* that a massive field of ice lay ahead directly in its path. The situation called for "vigilance, caution, and skill," but the *Titanic* was performing better than had been expected, and Captain Smith wasn't prepared to slow down, nor did he significantly alter course. He had confidence in his new ship, and steered it blindly towards the ice that he knew lay ahead.

At 9 a.m. the Roman Catholic Chaplain, Father Thomas Roussel Byles celebrated Mass. In his sermon he told those assembled that they must have a spiritual lifeboat in times of trouble. At 10:30, Captain Smith held an interdenominational Divine service in the First Class Dining Salon. There should have been a lifeboat drill afterward but Smith cancelled it perhaps because, as he once said, "I cannot imagine any condition that would cause a ship to founder. Modern shipbuilding has gone beyond that."

It was a calm, relaxing day. Two days left at sea, and passengers began making arrangements for their arrival in New York. Just before he went down for dinner, George Graham dropped into the wireless room to send a Marconigram off to his wife in Toronto: "New York Wednesday Morning. Wire me Sandy Hook. Well." Mark Fortune dropped into the wireless room too and wired the Belmont Hotel in New York. "Reserve two double rooms with bath and single. Arriving Wednesday." In his third class cabin, Neshan Krekorian played cards then crawled into his bunk. He didn't undress, just kicked off his boots, felt a draught, and noticed that a porthole was open. When he went to close it he peered out and saw icebergs on the water. "Even though it was the first time in my life I had seen ice flows I didn't think much of it because they were barely noticeable." Krekorian couldn't sleep because of the noise which could be heard even by first class passengers. There were complaints about "low class continentals who kept up loud conversations when they should be asleep and even indulged in singing and instrumental music."

At about the same time there was an impromptu hymn sing in the Second Class dining room. Norman Douglas, the Scots engineer, sat at the piano and played *Abide With Me* as Dr. Pain accompanied him on the flute. Marian Wright sang *Lead Kindly Light*, and Matilda Weisz contributed *The Last Rose of Summer*. Weisz thought she had performed well and that her rendition had "met with great success," but she seemed somewhat perplexed. After the hymn sing was over she joined her husband Leopold ✓ for a walk around the deck. But it had turned suddenly cold. The temperature had dropped to a killing minus one degree centigrade, and they didn't stay outdoors for long. There was something in the air, something rotten and penetrating, damp and unappealing. Matilda described it as a "clammy odour." She shivered as she headed inside.

"I do feel strange." she said.

"I guess we're in the ice," he shrugged.

Chapter Seven

MAJOR ARTHUR PEUCHEN sat down to dinner in the *Titanic*'s Jacobean dining room with Harry Molson and Hud and Bess Allison. The table was adorned with fresh daffodils, Royal Crown Derby china, crystal, and candlelight. It was so lovely Bess brought her daughter, Loraine, into the room for a few minutes so the little girl could see for herself how pretty everything was. "The dinner was an exceptionally good dinner," Peuchen would remember later. "It seemed to be a better bill of fare than usual, though they were all good." On the menu were plover eggs with caviar, oysters, soup, a choice of lamb, duck, chicken or beef, and an orange bombe with spun sugar.

The Fortune family dined together, and young Charles teased his father about the buffalo coat that been lugged half way around the world and back and that had never been used.

As Zette Baxter swept to their table on her brother's arm many in the room noticed, but were too polite to mention Zette's gaucherie: She wore a diamond and silver tiara. By 1912, tiaras were out-of-date. The only people who wore them were royalty—or vulgar colonials.

Bert and Vera Dick ate with Thomas Andrews who monopolized the conversation talking about his wife, his little girl, his mother, and family as well as his home in Belfast. At a table nearby, George Graham and four other salesmen, buyers for American chain stores, ended their meal by autographing each other's menus as souvenirs.

Somewhere in the background, rising above the idle chatter and seamless service, the orchestra played *The Tales of Hoffman*:

> Belle Nuit, O nuit d'amour
> Souris a nos caresses

Hudson and Bess Allison.
Militant evangelism was a constant presence in their lives.
Courtesy of Ella Deeks.

nuit plus douce que le jour
belle nuit d'amour.

It was an incredibly romantic evening. Everyone that night remembered the stars. Vera Dick recalled that "Even in Canada, where we have such clear nights, I have never seen such a clear sky." Clara Hays agreed the night was clear and the ocean "calm as a millpond." In his memoirs another passenger, Lawrence Beesley wrote:

> The sky without a single cloud to mar the perfect brilliance of the stars, clustered so thickly together that in places there seemed almost more dazzling points of light set in the black sky than background of sky itself; and each star seemed in the keen atmosphere, free from any haze, to have increased its brilliance tenfold and to twinkle and glitter with a staccato flash that made the sky seem nothing but a setting for them in which to display their wonder.

The complete absence of mist produced a phenomenon he had never seen before,

> where the sky met the sea the line was as clear and as definite as the edge of a knife, so that the water and the air never merged gradually into each other and blended to a softened rounded horizon, but each element was so exclusively separate that where a star came low down in the sky near the clear-cut edge of the waterline, it still lost none of its brilliance. As the earth revolved and the water edge came up and covered partially the star, as it were, it simply cut the star in two, the upper half continuing to sparkle as long as it was not entirely hidden, and throwing a long beam of light along the sea to us.

It was approaching 11 p.m. Many of the men had retired to the Louis Quinze smoking room. Major Peuchen left the dining room as the Allisons retired to their cabin and he wandered through the Palm Court before going into the smoking room where he found Beattie, McCaffry, and Austen Partner, enjoying cognacs, cigars, and scintillating conversation.

"Talk was unusually bright," Peuchen recalled. Talk surely would have been about politics and free trade with the United States. Six months earlier, in the Canadian general election, the Conservatives under Robert Borden had ended fifteen years of Liberal rule in Canada by opposing reciprocity with the United States. Had they been inclined to sports, they would have talked about hockey and the performance of the Quebec Bulldogs, who had just won the Stanley Cup. They might have made passing reference to the new sports car called a Bugatti that had made its appearance for the first time that year at the Grand Prix. They could have talked about Roald Amundsen's discovery of the South Pole; everybody that winter was talking about Amundsen. If they discussed popular fiction they would have mentioned Thomas Mann's *Death in Venice* and Gaston Le Roux's *Phantom of the Opera* which had just been published.

They laughed and talked and drank until bar service stopped and many excused themselves and went off to bed. But others lingered. Chevré joined aviation pioneer Pierre Maréchal, a Le Havre businessman, Alfred Omont, and Lucien "Clinch" Smith for a card game in the Café Parisien.

In spite of his name, Smith was a francophile, an American dilettante who maintained a pied-à-terre in Paris. (His brother-in-law was the renowned New York architect Stanford White, who was murdered on the roof of Madison Square Gardens by Harry K. Thaw in 1906.) In another alcove, Charles Hays relaxed with Colonel Archibald Gracie, a U.S. military historian from Washington, D.C., and with Edward Crosby, the Great Lakes shipping magnate who had a summer cottage on Georgian Bay. Cigar smoke hung like a blue shawl across their shoulders as they talked about ships and railroads and technological advances in transportation. At one point Hays conceded the *Titanic* was "a superlative vessel," but aware that the Germans were about to launch an even bigger passenger ship within one month he voiced his concern that the trend toward "playing fast and loose with larger and larger ships will end in tragedy."

"The time will come," he wagged his finger "when the race to build the fastest transatlantic ship will result in the greatest and most appalling disaster."

The *Titanic* plowed onwards at 22 knots through the darkness. Outside, reflected light from her portholes skipped like quicksilver across the calm surface of the onyx black sea.

Chapter Eight

11:40 p.m. A grey arctic glacier loomed into the surreal setting. It drifted silently, lethally, into the *Titanic*'s path and scraped the starboard side. Rivets beneath the *Titanic*'s water line popped. Hull plates buckled then snapped open. As the ship bumped along the side of the iceberg, chunks of ice fell on the starboard well deck around the foremast. Then, guided by the currents, the massive slab of ice slipped away into the darkness of the *Titanic*'s wake.

Chapter Nine

ALICE FORTUNE heard a faint metallic crunch and tried to gauge where the sound came from. In her second class cabin, Mrs. Weisz felt a tremor, "as if someone shook me roughly, no more than that." The Allison's cook, Millie Brown, shared her second class cabin with Mrs. Selena Cook, a British newly-wed on her way to America for the first time, who was travelling on the ship under her maiden name, Selena Rogers. The two women listened as three men had a pillow fight in the room next door. When the ship ran into the iceberg Brown jumped up: "Why, don't those boys make a noise!" she said, slightly annoyed. Then she heard "a horrid grating as though we had run into a lot of gravel, and then there was a terrible flush of water and the engines stopped." Paul Chevré was dealing a round of cards when he felt "a shock, a small one." Arthur Peuchen thought the ship had struck "an unusual wave. It was not like a collision and I didn't think it serious." He went out on deck briefly and watched the iceberg, 70 feet high, slip away. The ship glided to a halt. Then there was a deafening roar as steam rushed from the ship's exhausts "kicking up a row that would have dwarfed a thousand railway engines roaring through a culvert." A handful of passengers emerged from their staterooms, one by one, and gathered on deck, some in pajamas, some in evening gowns. No one was alarmed. Although the *Titanic* was dead in the water it seemed safe and secure. Someone idly speculated it had dropped a propeller. One supercilious steward suggested there was nothing to be afraid of. "We've sliced a whale in two," he said. "We'll be on our way again in minutes."

Twenty feet below the *Titanic*'s water line, torrents of water poured in. In ten minutes, seven feet of water flooded into the forward compartment. Even as passengers chatted, the *Titanic*'s head was being dragged down under the weight and imperceptibly the ship began to list to starboard.

Passengers in steerage had no doubt what was happening. Neshan Krekorian felt the ship "scud back, and tilt to one side. In a minute there was chaos and confusion," he said. "Women rushed hither and thither, and then the lights went out and we were all left in the dark. Everybody seemed to lose their heads and just stand about and shriek. Finally, in a minute or so the lights came on again and men seemed to be more cool than before. Lifebelts were taken from their places and nearly everyone put them on, but few of them were fastened properly." Krekorian rushed up the third class stairway and reached the deck. "Things were not so confused topside," he observed. "No one seemed afraid. They merely huddled in talking groups unaware that the ship was going down underneath them."

It was almost midnight. In the Café Parisien, Chevré thought it "too bloody cold" to leave his card game to venture outside to investigate. The temperature had dropped to just below freezing so he asked a steward to open a window and have a look. "When the waiter opened the port hole we saw nothing except a clear night," he said. Still, something had happened, and two of the card players, Chevré and Omont, fully expecting to return to their bridge game, pocketed the cards they were holding and decided to go out on deck and see what the fuss was all about. Clinch Smith hoisted his glass of Scotch. "If there is any ice on deck, I could use some in this," he chuckled as they all made their way outside.

In B-58, Hélène Baxter was in bed, sick with nausea. She found the throb of the engines relaxing, so when the *Titanic*'s propellers stopped churning at 11:45 p.m., she suffered an anxiety attack. Why, she wanted to know, was the *Titanic* stopping in mid-ocean? Why were the funnels blowing off steam? Minutes before midnight she dispatched her son, Quigg, to see what the commotion was all about. Quigg was more curious than alarmed as he stepped outside his stateroom at midnight. He saw Bruce Ismay, who occupied the neighbouring suite, conferring with the captain. Baxter wanted to know what was wrong.

"There's been an accident, Baxter, but it's all right," Captain Smith told him. "Nothing serious at all, go right back to bed." As Smith hurried away to the bridge, Ismay, his face as pale as the white night shirt he was wearing, was more forthright. He told Baxter that the ship had hit an iceberg, it was taking in water, and that the captain had decided to load the lifeboats.

Fifteen minutes later, the first wireless message asking for help was tapped out. Curiously, it did not convey any dramatic sense of urgency: "*Titanic* sends CQD. Requires Assistance. Position 41°44'N Longtitude, 50°24'N." Then, almost as an afterthought: "Come at Once."

At about the same time Captain Smith nervously "chewing on a toothpick," made his way to the bridge. Chevré bumped into him on deck and Smith told the French sculptor to put on his life preserver "as a precaution." Then Chevré watched as the crew uncovered lifeboat number 7 and begin working the davits. Chevré considered his options and didn't need to be told what to do next. He jumped in. So did his card-playing companions. "Some of the passengers shouted at us not to get in," said Omont, "As they had such confidence in the ship, but I saw that the sea was very calm, and on calm reason I thought it better to jump into the lifeboat and see what would happen."

The Fortune family had made their way up to the boat deck and were standing nearby. Even if getting into the boats was a precaution, Ethel Fortune thought the exercise a waste of time. Just as she was deciding what to do, she heard the ship's orchestra break into *Glowworm*. The snappy music convinced Ethel nothing serious had happened, so she left her mother and two sisters on deck and went back to the comfort of her cabin. Alice and Mabel were so unconcerned as they prepared to get into the boat they emptied their pockets, took off their jewellery and handed it to their brother, Charles, for safekeeping. "Look after father, Charles," they yelled as they watched their father come out on deck sporting his buffalo coat.

"See," he chuckled as he modelled the ratty fur, "I told you it would come in handy."

Back in her cabin, Ethel looked for her mother, but a steward informed her that Clara had joined Alice and Mabel in the boat. "He hurried me up to the side and I had to come down and jump into the boat. The people in

Ethel Fortune was in Europe shopping for a trousseau
for her marriage to Crawford Gordon.
Courtesy of Flora Brett.

Charles Alexander Fortune teased his father about
his Winnipeg buffalo coat.
Courtesy of Bishop's College School.

the boat caught me," she later said.

First Officer Murdoch called for more passengers to get in, but no one seemed interested, so Murdoch ordered the lifeboat to be lowered. Number 7 was the first boat on the starboard side to leave the ship. There were more men in it than women: sixteen men, three of them crew, and twelve women. Omont, who was in the boat thought even that was too many. "The idea of putting sixty people in a boat or on a raft is ridiculous," he harrumphed. "I consider it a monstrosity to state that one could put sixty people in such a boat safely."

The Dicks had been undressing, getting ready for bed, and felt nothing. They were interrupted by a rap on the door. It was the bedroom steward who had taken a shine to Vera. "I'm sure we would have slept through the whole thing, if a steward hadn't rapped on the door shortly after midnight and ordered us to put on our lifejackets." Bert Dick wasn't certain the steward knew what he was talking about so he went to find Thomas Andrews and asked Andrews what was happening. "It is very serious, but keep the bad news quiet," Andrews told him, "We don't want anyone to panic." The bedroom steward had to cajole Vera into putting on a life jacket. "Try this on for size," he laughed, "It's the very latest fashion, all the stylish people are wearing them."

Back in his cabin, C104, Arthur Peuchen grabbed three oranges and a pearl pin but ignored $200,000 worth of stocks and bonds, his jewellery, and the presents he had bought for his son and daughter. He certainly didn't believe the ship was going to sink. Peuchen thought it sad that he had to leave his "cheery room, cozy, large and comfortable as it was," to go up top. Peuchen caught up with Thomson Beattie, and asked Beattie what the fuss was all about. Hadn't he heard? "The order is for life belts and the boats," Beattie told him. Only then was Peuchen really aware that people in the companionways were wearing life preservers and distraught women seemed anxious. He continued up the grand staircase and saw Hugo Ross, still in his pajamas, poke his head around the corner.

"What's going on?" Ross asked.

"We've hit an iceberg and you'd better come out to the boat deck."

"Is that all?," Ross shrugged. "I'm sick. It will take more than an iceberg to get me off this ship."

One of the Allison's maids, Sarah Daniels, didn't realize the engines had stopped until a bedroom stewardess came into her cabin and told her to get dressed. "I was so sleepy that as soon as the maid left the room I got into bed again and only began to dress when another girl came round and aroused me. We all did as we were told. There was no excitement and not knowing what had happened we were not alarmed." There was no loud hailer or public address system to let anyone know the ship was crippled. No instructions were forthcoming. The other maid, Alice Cleaver, bundled up the infant in her charge, Trevor Allison, and with the baby in her arms, apparently went off to second class to round up the rest of the Allison household without telling anyone. Out on deck, with steam still roaring from the funnels it was impossible to shout above the uproar. The crew staggered up to man the boats but there had been no boat drill so most of them had no idea where to go.

In her second class cabin, the Allison's cook Millie Brown, couldn't believe anything serious had happened. She decided to go back to sleep. The Allison's young chauffeur, George Swane, knocked on her door, woke her, and urged her to dress and put on a life jacket. Selena Cook didn't want to put a preserver on at all. "It was awful to put the life belt on," she said. "It seemed as if you really were gone. Then came the lowering of the boats. I shut my eyes and hoped I should wake and find it a dream."

The dream was turning into a nightmare. The first real evidence that something was amiss was the appearance on the boat deck of about 100 grim-faced stokers with their dunnage bags. It was against the regulations, of course. Stokers were not permitted on the passenger decks and one of the ship's officers ordered the firemen below. They complied, and in the words of one witness were "driven like a lot of sheep" off the deck.

More and more people began to mill around, but not everyone seemed flummoxed. Wealth breeds a sense of invincibility. No one who pays good money to be pampered expects anything less. Few were prepared to abandon the warmth and comfort of a stateroom to be dangled down a

Major Arthur Peuchen, soldier and yachtsman.
"Surely we're not going to have that man," he said
when he learned E.J. Smith was the *Titanic*'s commander.
Photo from *Men In Canada*, 1901.

The Countess of Rothes.
The robust blueblood took control of boat #8.

sixty-foot drop. Everyone stood around in the cold, dumfounded, and quietly speculated what they should do. Quigg Baxter carried his mother up the grand staircase to the boat deck on the Port Side and lifted her into lifeboat number 6. Then he went and got Berthe Mayné, who slipped a long woolen motorcoat over her night dress, but balked when Quigg asked her into the lifeboat without him. She wanted to go back to her cabin to get some jewellery, she said. Denver socialite Molly Brown interrupted the two of them, and told Mayné to get into the boat. Quigg nonchalantly introduced Berthé to his bewildered mother and sister, and asked them to look after her.

"Quigg didn't seem at all disturbed," Zette would tell the Montreal *Standard*, "While he didn't relish being parted from us, he bade me farewell bravely." She also claimed Captain Smith was nearby as they got into the boat, and that he asked her whether her mother was comfortable. As Quigg helped them into number 6 he whipped a sterling-silver brandy flask out from inside his vest pocket, took a healthy swallow, and handed it to his mother.

"Here, you'll need this to keep warm on the open sea," he said.

His mother began to admonish him about his drinking, and he cut her short with an air of unruffled calm.

"Êtes-vous bien, Maman?" he interrupted her. He kissed her, kissed Berthé, and waving his goodbys he called "Au revoir, bon espoir vous autres." Then he stepped back from the rail and watched the second lifeboat leave the ship.

Major Peuchen looked over the ship's rail as number 6 was lowered. Peuchen was concerned because it was leaving empty and when he asked Second Officer Charles Lightoller why, he was told that the ropes would not hold a full load. At that point someone in the boat yelled, "We've only one seaman here. Can somebody give us a hand?" Officer Lightoller shouted for help.

Peuchen stepped forward and told Lightoller that he was a yachtsman who could handle a boat as well as anyone. Number 6 had already begun its descent, and Lightoller told Peuchen if he was as good a sailor as he claimed to be, he could get into the boat and join them. Captain Smith suggested Peuchen go one deck below and break one of the windows on the promenade to get into the boat. But Peuchen grabbed a rope, swung himself off ship and, hand-under-hand, slithered down 25 feet into the boat. As soon as he was aboard, the crewman in charge, the *Titanic's* lookout, Frederick Fleet, ordered Peuchen to help him get the rudder operating.

Lifeboats had drainage holes in them which had to be plugged before they were launched. "Get down and put in the plug, and be quick about it. This boat is going to founder," Fleet commanded. Peuchen thought Fleet meant the lifeboat was going to founder, not the *Titanic*. He did as he was told, grabbed one of the oars, and in his words, "We rowed away like good fellows."

The din of escaping steam stopped suddenly and an ominous silence engulfed the ship. Shots in the sky continued to explode at ten-minute intervals as distress rockets were fired from the bridge.

Bessie Allison was put into a boat with Loraine then looked around for her baby, Trevor. Neither the boy nor his nursemaid were to be seen. Allison refused to leave the ship without her son; she dragged Loraine out of the boat, and went looking for Trevor. What she didn't know, was that Alice Cleaver and the baby, were by now one deck below in second class on the opposite side and other end of the vessel being loaded into lifeboat 11.

There were no men in number 8 so the Countess of Rothes took charge of the twenty-three women in it and it was lowered away. The Countess was an expert oarswoman, thoroughly at home at the sea. There was, it seemed, a boat off the starboard side on the distant horizon, the running lights of a vessel on its way to the rescue. Captain Smith saw them, Colonel Gracie saw them, as did Colonel Astor, and Alfred Crawford, a steward in boat 8, saw them too. In fact, the Countess of Rothes thought the ship was so close she could land the women aboard it and return to the *Titanic* for another load.

The lights were tantalizingly close, no more than six kilometres distant. But as the women dipped their oars into the water the lights vanished.

Charles Hays certainly thought another ship was off in the distance.

The railroad baron behaved as if everything was perfectly under control. With a cigar butt clenched between his teeth he instructed his young secretary, Vivian Payne, and his son-in- law, Thornton Davidson, to get the ladies into boat number 3. "You and mother go ahead, the rest of us will wait here until morning," he told his daughter, Orian. "Don't worry. This ship is good for eight hours, and long before then help will arrive." Hays planned to go back to their staterooms and sort through their luggage to condense into two or three bags the personal effects he wanted transferred to the rescue vessel. Orian was so reassured by his demeanour she didn't even think of kissing her father or her husband, Thornton, goodbye.

Vera Dick clung to her husband. They were locked in an embrace when their bedroom steward nudged both of them into the boat. "I was pushed into the boat," Bert claimed, "And the next minute it was being lowered. The seaman in charge of the lifeboat, however, George Moore, told a slightly different story. "I was told by the first officer to jump in the boat and pass the ladies in, and when there were no more about we took in men. There were a few men passengers, but they got in after all the women and children." he said. There were thirty-two on board, including eleven crewmen. Two pet dogs also made it into the boat, a Pomeranian and an Egyptian Dragoman. As the boat swayed and jerked toward the water, the Dicks thought it would capsize and wondered whether it might not have been safer for them to remain on board.

Further aft on the Second Class Promenade Charles Pain, the young doctor from Hamilton, with friends Marion Wright and Douglas Norman, stood quiescent, and attentive as they watched the lifeboats on the starboard side sway in the davits. Number 8 was being lowered and Douglas thought that was worth a picture. He left to get his camera. At that moment a distress rocket burst above the ship with the blinding intensity of a portrait photographer's magnesium flash.

"Do you think we're in danger?" Wright asked Pain, as the light seared the sky.

"I don't think so," Pain replied.

The area around them was getting uncomfortably crowded with people

pushing and shoving so Pain suggested they had "better go round the other side. There aren't so many people there."

They slipped to port side, making their way through the narrow passage between the raised roof over the First Class Smoking Lounge and the dome over the rear first class entrance. They found themselves in front of boat number 9 which was nearly full. They watched as one cantankerous old woman stubbornly refused to get in. The officer in charge gave up arguing with her.

"Any more ladies? This way," he shouted.

Suddenly Pain was overwhelmed by the total sense of emerging chaos, and by the realization that he might never see Wright again.

"You had better run," Pain grabbed her hand. "Get into the boat."

Wright didn't bother to say goodbye. She, too, thought that she would be back on the *Titanic* before dawn.

Chapter Ten

GEORGE HANNAH, traffic manager of the Allan Steamship Company, was nearing the end of his shift at the company headquarters on the Montreal waterfront at the corner of Rue de la Commune and St. Pierre streets at 10:30 when the message arrived from the *Virginian*, one of the company's ships. The vessel, two days out of Halifax on its way to Liverpool had 18,000 barrels of perishable apples in its cargo hold and was asking Hannah for permission to change its course in mid-ocean to go to the aid of a ship 170 miles away. The *Virginian* had picked a distress signal from the *Titanic*, and wanted to know what to do about it. Hannah called his friend Edward Stranger, a marine reporter with the Montreal *Gazette* up the street. When Stranger got to the steamship company offices both took turns eavesdropping on the wireless messages being relayed from Cape Race. When Stranger heard the *Titanic* tap out "We Are Sinking Fast; We Are Putting The Women Off In Boats," he knew he was on top of a story. Then they lost the signal. Hannah surmised they wouldn't be able to hear anything more because the *Virginian* had changed its course and had sailed out of Marconi wireless range. "The next important message, if there is one, will come from some of the other ships in the area," he told Stranger.

By the time Montreal tuned in and learned what was happening at sea, eight lifeboats with 155 people aboard had already left the *Titanic*. There was room in those boats for 400. That left ten boats with room for another 600 or so still to be loaded. There were still 2,000 people on board.

Hannah and Stranger may have been close enough to monitor the drama, but they were too far away to be of help. At 12:27 a.m. Montreal time, Hannah picked up the last of the SOS signals until, as he said, they were cut off with great suddenness. Stranger was the first reporter in the world to learn of the sinking, but the scoop wasn't his alone. At the time the *Gazette* had a reciprocal news gathering arrangement with the *New York Times*, so the information Stranger was gathering for his paper in Montreal was relayed to the *Times'* managing editor, Carl Van Anda. Van Anda took a calculated risk and reasoned that if the ship was no longer sending out distress signals, it wasn't because the *Virginian* was out of range, but because the *Titanic* had gone down.

Back on board, the *Titanic*'s forward bulkhead collapsed and water spilled into boiler room number 5. Water from 5 began to spill into boiler room 6 and the ship's tilt grew noticeably steeper. Frank Maybery tripped as he started up the second class staircase. The stairs were leaning forward but there was no discernible slope—just enough of a tilt to throw his equilibrium off balance.

Passengers on the upper decks seemed calm but bit their lips, determined to carry on. After all, the odds of survival favoured those in first class. Of the twenty lifeboats, including the four collapsibles, twelve of them, with a capacity of at least 500, were immediately accessible to the 337 first class passengers from the Grand Stairway. The eight other boats which could carry 600 at most, were in the area aft reserved for the 1,000 people in second class and steerage. The irony was, the first class passengers were reluctant to get into their boats and those in steerage, desperate to get away, couldn't find their way to the boats. It wasn't easy for steerage passengers to get anywhere near them. First, they had to make their way up five decks through a maze of companionways and totally unfamiliar surroundings, then they had to navigate the second class stairwell before they found themselves on the boat deck.

Fifty or so immigrants, carrying bundles on their backs, got as far as the General Room on the Shelter Deck and didn't know where to go from there. They started to pray, slowly and desperately. The sound of the voices chanting the rosary, "Holy Mary, Mother of God, Pray for us sinners, Now and at the hour of our death," was irritatingly sepulchral to others around them. A few passengers ridiculed those who prayed and "started a ring dance around them."

Many people still didn't recognize the danger. One woman ushered into a boat took her seat, hesitated, looked around and found the surroundings physically uncomfortable. So she got out and disappeared down a companionway into a crush of passengers. Elias Nicola-Yarred, the twelve-year-old Syrian travelling without his parents "thought the excitement was a lot of fun. He scrambled up a ladder "like a little monkey," to get a better view. His guardian, an old man, clambered up after him, and put him in a boat. Then he went back for Elias' sister, Jamila, "who was heavy and hard to manage." But he got her in just as the boat was pulling away.

Evacuation procedures were improvised as they went along. Stewards hustled women to the boat deck, and when they got there other stewards sent them traipsing back one deck below to the enclosed promenade on A Deck where it was warmer. They were told to be patient, and instead of going up to the boats, were instructed to wait until the boats come down to them. It was all grossly inefficient.

The fantail deck was congested. Passengers waiting to be told what to do and where to go, crowded A Deck. Up on the boat deck, the officers promenade near the wheelhouse was almost deserted. Sir Cosmo Duff Gordon, his wife Lucille, and their maid Miss Francatelli, who hadn't followed instructions to wait below, thought it was a curiously quiet corner. Duff Gordon glanced around, saw only a few men standing around lifeboat number 1, and from his vantage point on the ship, presumed all the women were now off the boat. Sir Cosmo asked First Officer William Murdoch for permission to get in. "With pleasure. I wish you would." Murdoch, a bulldog of a man, was almost deferential. The Duff Gordons were a formidable couple, not the kind of peoplewho would have taken no for an answer. One of Gordon's cousins, Lord Aberdeen, had been the Governor General of Canada in the 1890s. Another cousin was Prime Minister of England in the 1850s. Gordon himself had fenced for the British in the 1908 Olympics. Lady Gordon was even better known than her husband— a fashionable dress designer who owned Madame Gordon of Hanover Square in London. She is said to have held the first fashion show to use live models on a ramp. They were on their way to Chicago where Lady Gordon planned to open a shop. Just as they stepped in to the boat, two men, Henry Stengel, a leather manufacturer from New Jersey, and Abraham Saloman, a New York businessman, wandered along. "Jump in," Murdoch barked at them. Stengel, taken by surprise, tripped and literally rolled along the deck on his side until he plopped into the boat. Murdoch roared with laughter. "That's the funniest thing I've seen all night," he said, and with that ordered number 1 to be lowered away. There were twelve people in it, including two sailors and five crewmen. As they began to row away they could sea the water begin to erase the giant white letters on the prow that spelled out the ship's name, *Titanic*.

Foreboding now turned to alarm. As number 10 was being jerked down from the port side with forty-one woman and seven children and four crewmen aboard, third class passenger Neshan Krekorian ran down the A deck, leapt, and landed in the boat. Able seaman Frank Evans, who was in charge of the boat, would later testify that the Armenian "deliberately jumped and saved himself."

Some *Titanic* enthusiasts say Krekorian stowed away in lifeboat number 6. It is highly improbable. Boat 6 left the ship before passengers from third class were allowed on the upper decks. Survivors themselves say the young man with the broken arm in number 6 was, in fact, ordered into the boat by Captain Smith, and was probably one of the Italian waiters from the First Class Dining Room. In his book, *A Survivor's Story*, Colonel Archibald Gracie insists the Italian in boat 6 was not a stowaway. When he tried to row, he couldn't because his arm was injured. Col. Gracie's story is corroborated by another passenger in the boat, Mrs. Churchill Candee.

For the most part, though, the boats continued to be filled in orderly fashion and without incident. Fifty-eight women and children from second and third class overcrowded number 11. An infant was tossed like a football to the officer in charge of number 13. He caught it.

At 1:30 a.m., the gates down below were unlocked and steerage passengers were allowed to pass directly through first class. Boats 12, 14, and 16 were lowered almost simultaneously. There were forty-three people aboard

12, more than sixty women in 14, and fifty women and children from second and third class in 16. Benjamin Hart saw his wife and daughter, Eva, off in number 14. "You'll be back on board for breakfast," he assured his wife. Then turning to his little girl, he said, "hold mummy's hand and be a good girl." As the boat was being lowered, a young teenage boy from second class, tried to force his way in. Harold Lowe, the officer in charge, grabbed him by the collar and shoved a revolver into his face. "I give you ten seconds to get back on to the ship before I blow your brains out," Lowe screamed at the terrified youngster. As the boy begged for his life, a little girl in the boat tugged at Lowe's sleeve and cried, "Oh Mr. Man, please don't shoot." With that the boy got out of the boat.

There weren't many teenagers travelling in second class; the boy may have been Alfred Gaskell, the sixteen-year-old barrel maker on his way to Montreal with Joseph Fynney, or perhaps it was eighteen-year-old-Joseph C. Nicholls, an Englishman travelling to the United States with his mother, Agnes Davis, and his stepbrother, John. Just as the teenager was thrown out, another man jumped into number 14 and had to be forcibly ejected. Although there was space for another passenger, Lowe thought he had overcrowded the boat and expected that "at any moment it would be doubled up under my feet." As the boat dropped one deck, Harold Lowe, the Fifth Officer in charge, saw a crowd of men "glaring like wild beasts ready to spring," so he fired his pistol to scare them "without the intention of hurting anyone." Number 13 had trouble getting away and had drifted directly under number 15, where it had become stuck. Fifteen started coming down on top of it, and threatened to crush the passengers in the boat below. At the last minute, someone cut the ropes and 13 shoved away as 15 landed in the water.

There were only a couple of boats left now, including Collapsible C. About two dozen men, variously described as "latinos," "dagoes," or "Italians," fought their way towards it. Those who managed to tumble into the boat were pulled from it by their legs, kicking. Mariana Assaf, one of the Syrians on her way to Ottawa, saw what happened: "There were many in steerage who tried to rush the boat and at those the captain and officers fired revolvers and some were shot dead," she said. "The rest were driven back. They were not given a chance to escape. I forgot everything and rushed up to the deck where the first class passengers were. When I ran up to the deck, I saw that the ship must be going to sink and I lost my head. But a man, I think he was one of the sailors, when he saw that, he pushed me into one of the boats where there were already many women and a few men. I felt that I was going to go crazy."

The perspective, of course, depended on one's social standing. Second class passenger Hilda Slayter of Halifax thought force was necessary to keep undesirable foreigners out of the boat. "Steerage men passengers had attempted to seize one of the lifeboats and there was a revolver fight," she said. "The prompt command of the officers restored order. There was a steady round of lively airs. It did much to keep up the spirits of everyone and considerably aided the efforts of the officers to prevent panic." The pistol shots were not fired by Captain Smith as Assaf thought, but by Officer Murdoch who ordered all the men in C to "Clear out." Then Bruce Ismay stepped into the Collapsible. No one told him to leave. No one dared to order the White Star Line's managing director out of one of his own boats.

Number 4, which had been hanging empty in its davits by the promenade windows on A Deck for more than an hour was finally loaded and cranked away. The ship was listing so badly that the lifeboat hung so far out from the side that a deck chair had to be used as a bridge for the forty-two first class passengers who clambered aboard. The *Titanic* was now deep in the water, so deep that the normal fifty foot drop from A Deck to the water was less than twenty feet. The orchestra had moved from the first class stairwell inside, out on the boat deck and continued to play. To those at the far end of the ship, the strains of a popular waltz, *Songe d'Autumn*, seemed distant but alive.

Harry Markland Molson took off his shoes and padded around the deck in his stocking feet. He was used to accidents at sea, and if he needed to swim he knew from experience that unnecessary footgear would hinder his efforts. He had already survived two shipwrecks. In 1899, Molson swam away from the sinking of the *Scotsman* in the Gulf of St. Lawrence, and in

1904, he swam to shore when the the the *Canada* collided with a collier in the St. Lawrence River near Sorel. At the time, the *Montreal Herald* reported he managed to don his shirt and trousers but no more. "He jumped through a stateroom window and a short time afterwards was picked up by a lifeboat. As soon as he was rescued from his own predicament he took a very active and helpful part in rescuing those still in the water." Molson was a strong swimmer and he could see the lights of a ship a point and a half off the port bow. He would have to swim three or four miles to safety, but he'd done it all before.

Bess Allison was in hysterics. By now it was obvious that if she couldn't find her baby boy, he must be safe in a boat with his nanny. But as her husband hustled her along the deck looking for a lifeboat to get his wife and daughter into, he was confronted by rows of empty davits. All the boats were gone. Shortly after 2 a.m., Lightoller began to fill the last collapsible raft, Englehardt D, and he couldn't find any women to put into it. There were no more women on the boat deck so men got in. When a few women came forward, the men got out and gave them their seats. Just then the *Titanic* lurched and the sea rolled up in a wave, washing over the bridge and driving people back. Those who didn't slip into the sea scampered frantically up the slanting decks towards the stern which was rising steadily as the bow went down. John Joughlin, the ship's chief baker, started heaving deck chairs overboard so that passengers already in the water might have something to cling to.

Thomson Beattie and Thomas McCaffry had to be on the roof beside the last available raft, Collapsible A, which was over the officers' quarters below the first funnel when the ship wobbled and began its slide. As the ship shuddered, a number of women already in the boat were thrown out of it, and when dozens of men tried to clamber aboard they swamped it. Those who managed to claw themselves into the boat found themselves standing in freezing water up to the gunwales. Beattie made it. McCaffry didn't.

There was a dull rumble as everything within the ship broke loose, a shattering report, then a scraping burst of metal. Any hope those still on board may have had for their lives evaporated into wails of unspeakable terror. The forward funnel broke loose and in a shower of sparks and soot crashed into water crushing to death those in its path. Floor after floor, the lights went out. One eyewitness described it like this: "Something in the very bowels of the *Titanic* exploded, and millions of sparks shot up to the sky. This red spurt was fan shaped as it went, but the sparks dispersed in every direction in the shape of a fountain of fire. Two other explosions followed." Then black mayhem. The *Titanic* snapped in two between the third and fourth funnels. Those still on deck were thrown into the appalling sea. Many of them wearing cork life preservers had their necks broken as they fell from the heights and hit the water. In the darkness the stern, now a perpendicular pillar, was outlined black against the stars. It bobbed a bit for almost five agonizing minutes and stood on end, defiant against the sky. Then almost furtively it began to slip into the sea, gathering speed as it went. The end was instantaneous. In one cold, paralyzing wave, the North Atlantic swallowed the liner. In a heartbeat, it was gone. All that remained was a wreath of floating, wailing bodies and flotsam circling the *Titanic*'s grave.

 People with broken limbs thrashed about, and those who couldn't swim gasped and struggled to breathe. Salt water choked them and the frigid sea dropped into their lungs like iron. Their last breath was water. Agonized screams dissolved into whimpering cries, then faded into moans that disappeared into the awesome silence of the dead.

Chapter Eleven

THEY DIDN'T TURN BACK.

The life boats headed north through the darkness into the wind. The survivors were traumatized, terrified and afraid that if they went back, those still thrashing about in the water in their death throes would swamp their boats. It is human nature for those who have survived a disaster to go into denial or to gripe about their circumstances, and survivors of the *Titanic* were no exception. In number 11, someone led the passengers in a cheer and everyone "cheered and cheered to drown the screams." In boat 13 passengers began to sing "Pull for the shore, sailor, pull for the shore!" so they couldn't hear the cries of the dying. In 14, they sang too, only the song was a hymn, "Throw out the life line, someone is sinking today."

The sound of their own voices reassured them that they were alive!

To seven-year-old Eva Hart it seemed as if "all at once everybody had gone, drowned, finished, the whole world stood still. There was nothing. Just this deathly, terrible silence in the dark night with the stars overhead." In boat number 7, Ethel Fortune was haunted by one last terrifying glimpse of her brother Charles in the water, "life jacket on, struggling to stay afloat." She couldn't possibly have seen him. It was too dark, so dark you couldn't tell who was seated next to you. Although the image of her drowning brother was almost certainly the product of her overheated imagination, the thought of Charles flailing about crying for someone to save him would stay with Ethel for the rest of her days.

In number 6, Major Arthur Peuchen asked helmsman Robert Hitchens to row back and look for survivors. Hitchens cut him short. His responsibility, he said, was to the living, not to the dying and the dead. "It's our lives now! Not theirs. There's only a lot of stiffs out there," Hitchens said.

Hitchens had seen Quigg Baxter give a brandy flask to his mother as he put her in the boat. He demanded she give him a swig from it. She gave him one, then started crying for her son. Her daughter Zette tried to comfort her. To Zette, the *Titanic* had gone easily and quietly, "as if it was the funeral of a sailor who had died at sea. But the cries of the people who went down with her were horrible to hear." She asked Hitchens to reconsider, but again, he refused to turn back. The women in number 6 were terribly uncoordinated. Major Peuchen suggested they might be better off if one of the women took the tiller from Hitchens so that he might help man the oars. The quartermaster thought Peuchen insubordinate: "I am in charge of this boat," Hitchens yelled. "It is your job to keep quiet and row." As a yachtsmen Peuchen understood the rule of the sea—you never second-guess the officer in charge. So he shut up. "I knew I was perfectly powerless," he said later. "Hitchens had been swearing a good deal and he was very disagreeable." When Hitchens suggested that they let the boat drift, Denver socialite Molly Brown, who could swear like a sailor herself, took charge. She began to row and showed the other women how. When Hitchens moved to stop her, the Unsinkable Molly told him if he didn't shut up she would throw him overboard. Hitchens shut up.

In number 5, which was tied to number 7, Third Officer Herbert Pitman wanted to pull towards the wreck. He had room for 60 in the two boats, but the people in the boats refused to obey his orders and sat on their oars. They drifted along and did nothing. Then Duff Gordon heard agonizing cries about 200 yards from their near empty boat number 1, and when fireman Charles Hendrickson proposed they turn back, Lady Gordon objected, so he didn't.

In number 8 the Countess of Rothes complained so much that seaman Thomas Jones gave her the tiller to keep her quiet, but the plucky countess continued to give everyone on board a running commentary. Jones pleaded with the women to turn back, and when they refused, he said, "if any of us are saved, remember, I wanted to go back. I would rather drown with them than be saved with you."

Five people managed to swim to boat number 4, and when it came along side number 14, the Fifth Officer, Harold Lowe, decided to transfer passengers from the overcrowded boats into the half-empty ones and go back to look for people in the water. Lowe rounded up five of the boats and tied them together to keep them from aimlessly drifting apart. He cursed as he lashed the boats together and worked to distribute the passengers evenly. Some women were offended by his blasphemies. He stared them down and ordered them "to take a nap!" Once 14 was emptied, Lowe turned back to see if anyone was still swimming. He was the only one who took the risk. He steered his boat through hundreds of bodies but it was so dark he couldn't tell which were alive and which were dead. His crew pulled a "corpulent gentleman" aboard, but the man was so heavy, so waterlogged, it took all hands to fish him in. He died shortly afterwards. They also picked up a steward and a second class Japanese passenger, Masabumbi Hosono, who had lashed himself to a door.

There hadn't been time to launch Collapsible B. As the ship went down the collapsible floated free and capsized. Second Officer Charles Lightoller had gone down with the ship, and couldn't recall how he wound up alive on the overturned collapsible, but as senior officer he was in charge. People stood upright, balancing themselves all night. Lucky Lightoller was convinced that his devout belief in Christian Science had once again saved him and thought it a miracle that anyone on the boat survived. "If ever human endurance was taxed to the limit, surely it was during those long hours of exposure in a temperature below freezing, standing motionless in our wet clothes. We were painfully conscious of that icy cold water slowly creeping up. Some quietly lost consciousness, subsided into the water, and slipped overboard." Two dozen managed to sit on the overturned boat and as they hung on through the night they recited the Lord's Prayer.

In number 3, Clara Hays kept shouting for her husband. Whenever she heard a noise, she cried, "Charlie, are you there Charlie Hays?"

Survivors in Collapsible A drifted aimlessly for hours until Lowe spotted them. He hauled them into number 14, but left three bodies behind in the Collapsible. One of the dead was Thomson Beattie.

"Are you sure they are dead?" Lowe asked.

"Absolutely sure," came the reply. Someone draped lifebelts over the faces of the three corpses and the boat was set adrift.

Thomson Beattie's death was described in detail by Ole Abelseth, a twenty-six-year-old Norwegian who was hauled into the life raft after the ship went down.

"It was just at the break of day, and he was lying down and seemed to be unconscious, he was not really dead and I took him by the shoulder and raised him up, so that he was sitting up. He was just sitting down, right on the deck, and I said to him, 'We can see a ship now, brace up.' And I took one of his hands and raised it and shook him, and he said, 'Let me be, Who are you?' I held him up like that for awhile, but I got tired and cold, and I took a little piece of small board, a lot of which were floating around, and laid it under his head on the edge of the boat to keep his head out of the water; but it was no more than a half an hour or so when he died."

The Fortune sisters rowed with their blistered hands until dawn came and the sea turned choppy. As the sky turned a pale pastel pink, they found themselves surrounded by mountains of ice. To one lady, the icebergs looked like "giant opals." To another, it seemed the boats were in a never-ending meadow covered with new fallen snow." Arthur Rostron, captain of the Cunard liner, *Carpathia*, racing to the rescue 58 miles from the southeast, counted at least two dozen icebergs, at least 200 feet high, and dozens more smaller ones. In the early morning light he thought they resembled "minarets, like cathedral towers turned to gold, and here and there some seemed to shape themselves like argosies under full sail."

Boat 13 was the first to spot the *Carpathia*'s mast lights and its single red and black stack. The *Carpathia* was no *Titanic*. A small, unpretentious ship, it was designed for the Hungarian immigrant trade between Fiume and New York. At 13,600 gross tonnes, it could accommodate 1,900 passengers. It had been eastbound heading for Gibralter with only 473 passengers aboard when it picked up the *Titanic*'s distress signals. Orian Davidson took off her straw hat and put a match to it to attract the *Carpathia*'s attention. The agony, the uncertainty was over, and many in the lifeboats burst into uncontrolled sobs of relief. At 5 a.m., the 705 survivors began to be taken aboard.

Simon Senecal of Montreal was a passenger on the *Carpathia* as the *Titanic*'s passengers were hauled to safety. He scanned the horizon, still fully expecting to sight the *Titanic* at any moment.

There was not one of us on board who believed the largest ship in the world was in any serious position. The officers, too, while we were speeding to the scene of the destruction absolutely refused to believe that the *Titanic* could sink and it was only in the early daylight seeing the lifeboats coming toward us and the wreckage floating round that we realised the awful catastrophe. It was only when the first passenger from the lifeboats who was in a fit state of mind to speak reached our decks from the sling seat that we had witnessed the most terrible marine accident ever recorded. How can I describe it to you? It was an unending procession of misery. Half clad women, some with children, others moaning and wailing over the loss of loved ones, all bearing the stamp of having endured suffering and privation indescribable. It is too terrible.

Boat 6 was the last to be emptied. Zette Baxter was indignant because one woman "absolutely refused to be hauled up unless her dog was taken up first. She had the dog in her muff and she absolutely refused to go up 'till that dog went up. Dogs were saved when good men drowned." The first thing Zette did aboard the *Carpathia*, was to cable to her husband, Dr. Douglas, in Montreal: MEET STEAMER CARPATHIA, CUNARD LINE, THURSDAY, NEW YORK WITH JAMES.(Her eldest brother). She also tried to dispatch another message, SAVED. WIRE US IF HEAR FROM QUIGG. but the wireless operator was so swamped the message was never sent.

Millie Brown couldn't afford to send a wireless message, so she sat down and wrote her mother a letter on four pages of lined foolscap:

On board the *Carpathia*, April 17, 1912
My dear mother, at last I have made myself sit down to write

to you. I don't know how the time has gone since the wreck but I can't help thinking how lucky I am to be among the rescued. There were 2,000 people—about that—on board and only about 700 saved. It happened at 11:30 on Sunday Night. Our ship ran into an iceberg and within an hour and half the vessel sunk. I couldn't believe it was serious and wouldn't get up until Swane came and made me, that was the last I saw of him, poor fellow. No sooner was I on deck than I was bustled to the First Class deck and pushed into one of the boats, and I found nurse (Alice Cleaver) and the baby (Trevor Allison) there. Then came the lowering of the boat. I shut my eyes and hoped I should wake and find it a dream. Then came the awful suspense of waiting till a vessel should pass our way. The wireless telegraph had been used and this vessel which was southward bound came miles out of its way to pick us up. By the time we had got out of reach of the suction we stopped to watch her go down, and you could watch her go too. It went in the front until it was standing like this \ and all the lights went out.

Shortly after we heard the engines explode and then the cries of the people for help. Never shall I forget it as long as I live. I daren't let myself think of it. We were on the water from 12 till 6 in this small boat. Thank goodness it was a clear, calm night or I don't know what would have happened. We were nearly frozen as there were icebergs all round us. Ever since I been here I've felt in a stupor, everything seems too much trouble, and I can't bother what happens to one. I found Sallie (Sarah Daniels) had got on all right but poor girl she keeps worrying about her things. Of course, we have lost everything but what we could stand up in. I had my watch on my arm. In fact it has never left it since we sailed, and my money was in my pocket.

I have not seen Mr. and Mrs. Allison or Loraine, so I suppose they have gone under. But there is just the chance they might have been picked up by another ship. I'm not going to worry about it as they have several friends on board and then there are all the partners of the firm. We have been offered a home until something is found for us. I have slept on the dining room floor for both nights, and we had a most awful thunderstorm last night and today it's that foggy I shall be glad to be on terra firma again. We had a bad start. The *New York* broke adrift and ran into us at Southampton. Well, I won't write any more now…don't worry about me as I shall be well looked after and I've made several well-to-do friends on board.

Lots of love to all, from your loving daughter, Millie.

Chapter Twelve

PEOPLE AWOKE that cataclysmic Monday to hear newsboys on streets across Canada hawk papers with cruelly contradictory headlines. In Montreal, the *Gazette* proclaimed TITANIC IN DANGER, and, reading between the lines, left little doubt that the ship had sunk. The *Daily Star*'s first edition, however, insisted TITANIC STILL AFLOAT; the second edition assured readers, WHITE STAR OFFICIALS CERTAIN TITANIC IS STILL SAFE. News spread by word of mouth, drawing large crowds to the White Star Lines Montreal office in the Bank of Commerce building on St. James street where the company's district manager, James Thom, told reporters that while the ship had been badly damaged, it was still afloat. "Twenty boatloads of passengers have already been transferred to the *Carpathia*, and allowing the capacity of forty to sixty in each boat, about eight to twelve hundred people have already been transferred," he said. "The *Baltic* and *Virginian* are near the scene, and the Allan liner *Parisian* is close at hand. While badly damaged, the *Titanic* is still afloat. I believe the steamer is unsinkable. But of course it must be very ugly for a steamer to have her bow knocked in."

According to Thom, the first passengers off the *Titanic* were being taken to Halifax, and would be brought by train to Montreal so they "could carry on and proceed to their various destinations." Based on Thom's assurances, the *Daily Star*'s noon edition hit the streets—TITANIC IS REPORTED SINKING: DISABLED VESSEL IS IN BAD SHAPE AND TOWS ARE TRYING TO KEEP HER AFLOAT TILL SHALLOW WATER IS REACHED. The French-language newspaper, *La Presse*, also held out hope with its headline: UN DRAME EN PLEINE MER: Le *Titanic* est sur un abîme: On annonce tous les passagers ont été sauvés a 3:30 a.m. The *Winnipeg*

LA CATASTROPHE DU "TITANIC"

1302 passagers manquent à l'appel. — Les seuls rescapés du naufrage au nombre de 868, sont sur le " Carpathia "

Le capitaine du navire français la " Touraine " avait signalé au " Titanic " la présence d'icebergs

LE MONDE ENTIER EST DANS L'ANGOISSE

| 1302 passagers manquent à l'appel | Les banquises sont la terreur des marins | La nouvelle cause un vif émoi en France | LES SURVIVANTS | Pénible défilé aux bureaux de la White Star | L'affolement dans Londres depuis hier |

Voici la liste des passagers recueillis à bord du " Carpathia "

PREMIÈRE CLASSE

Un avertissement de la "Touraine"

Ils ressemblent aux régions polaires

DEUXIÈME CLASSE

SURVIVANTS DONT LES NOMS NE SE TROUVENT PAS SUR LA LISTE DU " TITANIC "

Les règlements maritimes

Dix citoyens de Winnipeg

L'opinion d'Albert Ballin

Une législation préventive

14 chaloupes seulement

Le " Minia " n'avait pas de nouvelles

Le Devoir (Montreal), April 17, 1912.

Tribune told readers: PASSENGERS ARE REMOVED IN LIFEBOATS, and in Calgary the *News Telegram* flatly stated: MARINE DISASTER PREVENTED BY MEANS OF WIRELESS: VESSELS SPEEDING TO AID DISTRESSED LEVIATHAN. PASSENGERS REMOVED IN SAFTEY. The *Vancouver Sun* didn't bother to carry anything at all.

Judge Peers Davidson cabled London for information, and misinterpreted the garbled reply. White Star cabled a partial list of names of those aboard the *Carpathia*, but instead of prefacing the wireless message with the words "Those Saved," then listing the names, it began: ALL SAFE. Davidson didn't wait for the rest. He read what he wanted to and informed the world of the good news.

In Toronto, Edith Graham heard the news Monday morning, but her initial anxiety about the fate of her husband turned to relief when a wireless message arrived at 240 Dufferin Street. She had no way of knowing that it was sent before the ship went down. Mrs. Graham called Sandy Hook and was assured that a Mr. Graham was on the list of survivors. Eaton's sent a delegation to New York to meet him, but when it arrived it discovered their salesman was not on the survivor's list, but among the dead.

Prime Minister Robert Borden was on vacation in Hot Springs, Virginia, when he heard of the sinking. In Ottawa, the acting prime minister, George Eulas Foster, Minister of Trade and Commerce, caught wind of the story and immediately cabled Canada's High Commissioner in London, Lord Strathcona, three times in six hours to get more details. Strathcona was the dean of London's diplomatic corps, but was unable to learn anything. The language of his cabled replies reveals his frustration.

> White Star Line cannot furnish list Canadian passengers *Titanic*. So far as we are able to gather up to present following comprises all Canadians on board but there may be others: T McCaffry of Vancouver, Hugo Ross, Winnipeg, Major Peuchen, Toronto, Mr. and Mrs. Allison, Miss and Master Allison and maid, Montreal, Mr. and Mrs. Mark Fortune and three misses Fortune and Mr. Charles Fortune, Winnipeg, and Mr. and Mrs. Charles M. Hays, Miss and maid, Thornton Davidson, Montreal, and Markland Morrison, Montreal.

As the day progressed White Star officials proved to be uncooperative.

White Star Line were unable to furnish me with the names of Canadian passengers, the documents containing this information being on the vessel. In these circumstances the information was collected from such sources as available, and one or two slight errors have arisen, it now being uncertain whether the Allison family were Canadians. I am also informed that the Miss Hays whose name was given is not a relative of Mr. Charles M. Hays.

It wasn't until late Monday night that rumours about the full extent of the disaster began circulating and gained credence.

"A terrible thing happened today—the sinking of a boat which causes a lot of despair," Lady Marie-Louise LaCoste, the wife of Quebec's retired chief justice, Sir Alexander LaCoste, wrote in her diary Monday night. "The *Titanic* sank after hitting an iceberg without rescue, 2,000 people were on board, six or seven hundred were saved but separated from their friends and sons. Everyone is saddened by such unexpected news."

When the acting prime minister, George Foster, learned of the magnitude of the disaster, he immediately dispatched condolences to Number 10 Downing Street and to the White House. "The heart of all Canada beats in deepest sympathy," Foster said simply.

It wasn't until Tuesday morning, however, that newspapers everywhere carried the story. DOOMED LEVIATHAN TITANIC HAS FOUNDERED WITH 1400 SOULS ON BOARD: WORST MARINE DISASTER IN HISTORY STIRS TWO CONTINENTS, declared *the Ottawa Journal*. MONSTER WHITE STAR LINER FOUNDERS, proclaimed the *Halifax Herald*. The Duchess of Connaught confided with certainty to her diary on Tuesday, "Heard last night's rumour confirmed that the White Star Liner *Titanic* has foundered after a collision with an iceberg! 1,304 lives lost in her they say. She was the second of the two largest steamers afloat in the world! It is too horrible an accident for words to express." Ottawa journalist Ethel Chadwick, who covered the vice-regal court at Rideau Hall also noted the catastrophe in her diary: "They say 1,200 people were killed in the disaster to the steamer *Titanic*, the White Star Line today. A lot of prominent people were on board—W.T. Stead, a writer; John Jacob Astor, the Hays' of Montreal, Davidson, etc. I don't suppose any of them are saved. It is awful."

Flags on the Château Laurier Hotel were lowered to half mast. The A.E. Rea and Company on Sussex Drive installed a large color photograph of the *Titanic*, draped in black crepe with the Union Jack in one of its windows. "Hanging purple flowers are to the top of the window space and the whole window is in splendid accord and fitting to the catastrophe," the *Citizen* assured its readers. "The photoengravure shows the *Titanic's* great outlines and gives one a good idea of what a monster it must have been."

In Montreal, Mayor Louis-Arsène Lavallée was stunned by the loss. "Though as it appears the United States has suffered more grievously than Canada in this calamity, the citizens of Montreal have their share of sorrow," Lavallée said in a prepared statement. "Montreal will fly its flags at half-staff in a display of sympathy and sorrow." Goodwin's Department Store, on St. Catherine Street at the corner of University Avenue placed a seven foot arrangement of white chrysanthemums and carnations fashioned into an anchor in what was advertised as "one of the largest floral pieces ever made in Canada."

News of the disaster proved to be too much for J. P. Alexander, a former member of the Manitoba Legislature. "J.P. Alexander, registrar of the Boissevan land titles office dropped dead this morning after he got in a barber's chair. The news of the loss of the *Titanic* upset him, and the later news that his friend Hugo Ross was lost caused his death."

The *Vancouver Sun,* which missed the story completely on Monday, made up for it on Wednesday, April 17, with an evocative headline: WHERE ONCE WAS JOY AND LIGHT, OCEAN SPREADS WINDING SHEET OVER FATHOMLESS SEPULCHRES. Those who saw divine retribution behind the sinking had celestial evidence. That same day the moon slid across the sun's face and there was a total solar eclipse. All of North America was plunged into a weird and instant nightfall. Then it began to rain. On

Thursday the names of the survivors were confirmed, and by Friday, the downpour was so relentless it seemed that even Heaven wept.

"Torrential rains again today," Lady Lacoste wrote on Friday, April 19.

The newspapers officially reported that the *Titanic* did sink and that 1,600 people drowned. Among them we've lost our friend Mr. Hays, president of the Grand Trunk, with whom we had dinner for the last time when we were all together with the Duke of Connaught at the Governor General's residence. His wife and daughters are safe, as is the daughter of Judge Davidson, who are also friends of ours. The story of this terrible episode is very moving. So much despair, So much anxiety! We are all devastated by this terrible event. How small and ineffectual we are compared to He who orchestrates every event.

Prime Minister Borden returned from his holiday the following day, and cabled Strathcona in London: "This appalling disaster has brought sorrow to a great many households in Canada, and the United States and Great Britain as well. It will, however, undoubtedly bring about great improvement in the means of safeguarding human life." At Rideau Hall, the Governor General, Prince Arthur, in a letter to his nephew, King George V, wrote, "The loss of the *Titanic* sent a great thrill of horror and sorrow throughout this continent. I am happy to say very few Canadians lost their lives, and amongst these I believe only one woman. Most of the Canadians belonged to Montreal, to which city I sent my subscription (to aid the victims) and if not required there it will be sent to the Lord Mayor's fund; there is no central Canadian fund. I fear the ship, with its unwieldy length and great power was proceeding too fast for night with ice about."

Eaton's in Winnipeg closed its department store for one-half day in memory of George Graham. A memorial service for the dead was held at the Opera House in Vancouver. "Fully an hour before the time for the commencement of the service the Opera House was packed from floor to ceiling, and the stage scenery had to be removed to accommodate the crowds that kept pouring in," the *Sun* reported. "Hundreds were disappointed, unfortunately. Naturally on such an occasion the service was impressive as possible and even though in one or two instances there were outbursts of applause it was the outlet of the pent-up feeling of the huge gathering, feelings that were indicated by the dimmed eyes." The same Sunday mass was said for Quigg Baxter at Saint Patrick's Church in Montreal. During the service the pastor, Gerald McShane, made delicate and touching illusion to the lamented president of the Grand Trunk Railway. A similar service was held for Harry Markland Molson and Vivian Payne at Christ Church Anglican Cathedral. A brass tablet to Payne's memory was later erected in the cathedral by "123 of his associates."

Society reporter Madame La Bavarde summed it all up in her column in the *Montreal Standard.* "Seldom, if ever, has Montreal experienced a gloomier week. The social world has been at a standstill. With the uncertainty of the fate of the numerous Montrealers on board the ill fated *Titanic* unknown for several days, people in society were not inclined to do anything of importance in the way of entertaining. The numerous dinner parties arranged ... were cancelled."

It didn't take long to exploit the sinking. By Monday there were already those who were able to make money from it. That day the *Ottawa Citizen* carried an advertisement "Tonight at the Family Cinema—Pictures of the wreck of the *Titanic*, with a lecture explaining everything."

Chapter Thirteen

THE STATUE OF LIBERTY was wrapped with rain as the *Carpathia* made its way up the Hudson River through a thunderstorm the evening of Thursday, April 18, and angled its way to Pier 54 where the survivors, dazed with pain, came ashore. In spite of the miserable weather, there was a crowd of 30,000. Once they landed they found themselves victims of more confusion. They had to fight their way through a crush of what Dr. Fred Douglas described as "well meaning but useless people and morbid people who were using all sorts of influence to get close to us." To make matters worse, they were alarmed by what, to their raw nerves, seemed to be a bomb exploding. It was only a newspaper photographers flash but, as Douglas told *The Standard*, "it certainly made us jump."

The *Ottawa Journal* sent twenty-three-year-old reporter Grattan O'Leary to cover the story of the *Carpathia*'s arrival. In his memoirs, *Recollections of People, Press and Politics*, the future senator noted the assignment was not a tribute to his reporting ability, "but was based on the assumption that because I had spent several years at sea I was well qualified to interview survivors of a shipwreck." O'Leary arrived in New York during the driving rain, and stayed at the Breslin Hotel. There were, he writes, newspapers on the streets saying the *Carpathia* would not dock until the following morning, so he enjoyed a leisurely dinner with a couple of cocktails only to find out when he came out after dinner a later extra edition contradicted the earlier one and the *Carpathia* was on the point of discharging her pitiful survivors.

> I was anxious to get down to the docks and get the story, the most gripping of the day. When I arrived at the dock area it was

crowded with thousands of people eager to see who had escaped the most dramatic sea catastrophe in history. I had no police pass, and without it there was no way of getting through. I took a taxi to Associated Press, told the night editor who I was and what I was there for, and got his assurance that the first reporter to return from the docks would allow me use of his press pass. AP had 40 people out on the story and one of them was bound to come in at any minute. Sure enough, in about 15 minutes a reporter came into the office, and good as his word, the night editor, an upstanding Irishman, took the badge off his own man and turned it over to me. In a few minutes I was on my way through tight packed crowds miserable in the rain, many of them hoping for word of loved ones.

O'Leary's account appeared in the *Journal* on Friday, April 19.

The uniforms of two hundred nurses and Red Cross attachés mingled in the picture with the trim garbs of the ambulance surgeons and the chaste costumes of the sad faced sisters of charity. Ten score city policemen guarded the rope cordon lighted up at intervals with green lanterns whereby the guardians of the city's peace kept back at a distance of 75 feet the throng that kept pressing over-eagerly toward the pier where the *Carpathia* was docked. Within the shelter of the pier sheds were huddled nearly a thousand of the friends and relatives of the rescued and the lost. Many of them were weeping and sobbing without restraint. Outside in the murk and drizzle of the forbidding night stood ominous lines of ambulances to which nearly all the hospitals in the city had contributed their quota.

Pandemonium erupted as the survivors disembarked and were jostled by reporters, photographers, and anxious friends and relatives. No one could get near Alice Cleaver, who fended off reporters by telling them her name was Jean. She pressed Trevor Allison to her breast like a protective

The survivors arrive in New York.
Dr. Douglas meets Bertha Mayné (in hood), his wife Zette
with his brother-in-law James Baxter (holding suitcase).

shield and refused to let anyone take the baby from her. Vera Dick was more cooperative. She breathlessly told reporters how the lifeboat she was in frantically rowed from the *Titanic*. "It was those with the most brains who seemed to control themselves the best," she observed. "We were perfect fools not to have realized the danger long before we did. None of us realized our danger until the last moment. I saw the ship sink. All the while it went down the band played 'Nearer My God to Thee' and the men by the rail were splendid, splendid." Vera imagined the music in her head but her account struck a note with reporters and contributed to the definitive legend.

The next day there was a sensational eyewitness report of the disaster purporting to be by Paul Chevré. According to the story, Chevré was playing bridge in the smoking room at the time of the collision. Chevré was quoted as saying it was a "submerged berg, as I saw no sign of it afterwards, though the water was covered with floating ice." That part was true. Then it continued:

Captain Smith got the band back to the big dining room to play when the *Titanic* struck. They had finished their evening program some time before. Mr. Chevré saw that the lowering of the boats which took along the people on the ship appeared to be not appreciating the danger they were in. Chevré said an officer asked him to get into a life boat "to set an example." This he did and was followed by five or six girls, two of whom he believed were the missess Fortune of Winnipeg. Before the boat was anywhere near capacity it was dropped into the water and began to drift away. Suddenly the giant steamer gave a lurch over on its side and the lights went out. Then a frightening series of cries and screams were heard above the music which changed to *Nearer My God to Thee* at the last. Mr. Chevré then stated that a few minutes before the ship sank, Captain Smith cried out, "My luck has turned," and then he shot himself with a revolver he had been holding to use in case the men attempted to storm the boats before the women and children got away safely. I saw him fall against the canvassed railing on the bridge and disappear.

The story also quoted Chevré as saying that his bust of Sir Wilfrid Laurier destined for the lobby of the Château Laurier had been lost in the sinking. It was a dramatic read but complete fiction. Either the reporter didn't understand French, or simply made up the whole thing. Chevré was back in Montreal on April 22, and stormed into to *La Presse* to set the record straight. Everything that had been written about him in the English papers, he said, "was a tissue of lies." He had no idea how Captain Smith died because he was nowhere near the *Titanic* when it sank, and Laurier's bust did not go down with the ship.

"The marble bust with its pedestal and other accessories stands seven feet tall, and weighs 7,445 pounds. How do you think I could have had it in my cabin? Good lord! The bust is safe. It is actually aboard the *Bretagne*," he said. The sculpture was indeed in place for the hotel's opening on July 1, and still stands in the lobby of the Château Laurier Hotel in Ottawa. The *Herald* which printed the original Chevré interview insisted that its story "was certainly not faked," but allowed that because its reporter didn't speak French very well he "might have misinterpreted Mr. Chevré's rapid fire narrative."

The *Hamilton Spectator*, too, cobbled together a story that it claimed was an interview with Neshan Krekorian. It appeared on April 25. In the story, the reporter had Krekorian in the same boat as Major Peuchen, number 6, but it quoted Krekorian as saying that he and his companions crawled into a boat and hid under the thwarts until "one of the officers noticed the legs of one of us protruding from under the compartment and fished him out by the feet and threw him violently down upon the deck. Then he came to my end of the boat and grabbed the feet of two of my companions."

They too were taken out of the boat and chided for their cowardice. "They didn't see me and I remained where I was." If true, that meant Krekorian was in Collapsible A, from which stowaways were pulled. But

Peuchen wasn't in it and the collapsible was nowhere near the fantail top deck where Krekorian said he was. He is also quoted in the *Spectator* as saying "torches burned in the boat through the night to guide the rescuing vessel," another obvious fantasy.

Clara Hays was back in Montreal for the birth of her grandson on April 23. The boy was delivered without complications and was christened Thornton Davidson for his uncle lost at sea.

Loraine and Trevor Allison. The Allisons' servants arrived in Montreal with baby Trevor one week after the disaster.
Courtesy of Ella Deeks.

The Allison servants, Alice Cleaver, Sarah Daniels, and Millie Brown arrived in Montreal with baby Trevor one week after the disaster. "We landed in an awful thunderstorm when we were met by the Allison relations," Millie Brown wrote to her mother,

> Such a number of them—and by the way, Mr. and Mrs. and Loraine are really drowned—so we are staying at Mr. Allison's brother's

house. They all had a whimper and made a fuss about the baby. We caught the 8:40 train from New York to Montreal where we arrived 12 hours later. I must say I thoroughly enjoyed the ride, as the scenery was grand. We followed the Hudson River for quite a distance and the mountains on each side were splendid … it reminded me very much of *Ivanhoe* or *The Deerslayer*. When we arrived at the station, Mr. Allison's partners met us. Then we had a taxi to a hotel where we stayed the night (The Windsor). There were 14 stories and we were on the 8th. By the way this was the first time I had slept in a bed since the Saturday night. I gave vent to my feelings and had a good "laugh" you know. I had had to keep it in so long. We had been travelling with the others and had to keep ourselves in.

Chapter Fourteen

TWO DAYS AFTER the sinking of the *Titanic* the cable ship *Mackay-Bennett* with embalmers and an Anglican priest aboard, and the *Minia*, were dispatched from Halifax to gather the dead. When they arrived at the scene of the disaster bodies littered the ocean "like a flock of white sea gulls at rest on the sea." John Snow Jr., one of the embalmers on board was appalled with what he saw. Among the bodies dragged from the sea was that of a two-year-old boy. "He came floating towards us with a little upturned face, the only body recovered without a life belt," Snow told the *Halifax Herald*. "Nothing I saw at sea made such an impression on me. We found fifty bodies all in a group. A nearby lifeboat had capsized. There was a red skirt tied to a stick with which it is supposed that those in the boat had sought to attract attention, and failing, had gone down to their terrible deaths." Snow also thought it remarkable that "all of the watches worn by the men stopped at precisely ten minutes past two, to the second. There was not the very slightest deviation."

The *Mackay-Bennett*'s cable engineer, Frederic A. Hamilton, kept a diary of the gruesome mission:

> April 17, 1912
> Having taken in a supply of ice and a large number of coffins, cast off ... The Reverend Canon Kenneth Hind of All Saints Cathederal, Halifax, is accompanying the expedition; we also have an expert embalmer aboard.

> April 19, 1912
> The fine weather which has prevailed until now has turned to rain and fog.

April 20, 1912

A large iceberg, faintly discernible to our north, we are now very near the area where lie the ruins of so many human hopes and prayers. The embalmer becomes more and more cheerful as we approach the scene.

April 21, 1912

The ocean is strewn with a litter of woodwork, chairs and bodies, and there are several growlers about…The cutter lowered, and work commenced and kept up continuously all day, picking up bodies. Hauling the soaked remains in saturated clothing over the side of the cutter is no light task. Fifty-one we have taken on board today, two children, three women and forty-six men, and still the sea seems strewn. With the exception of ourselves, the Bosun bird is the only living creature here.

8 p.m. The tolling of the bell summoned all hands to the forecastle where thirty bodies are ready to be committed to the deep, each carefully weighted and each carefully sewn up in canvas. It is a weird scene, this gathering. The crescent moon is shedding a faint light on us, as the ship lays wallowing in the great rollers. The funeral service is conducted by the Reverend Canon Hind, for nearly an hour the words "For as much as it hath pleased the Lord, … we therefore commit this body to the deep," are repeated, and at each interval comes, splash! as the weighted body plunges into the sea, there to sink to a depth of about two miles. Splash, splash, splash!

April 22, 1912

We stormed past the iceberg today and endeavoured to photograph it, but rain is falling and we do not think the results will be satisfactory. All around is splintered woodwork, cabin fittings, mahogany fronts of drawers, carvings, all wrenched away from their fastenings, deck chairs, and then more bodies. Some of these are 15 miles distant from those picked up yesterday. 8 p.m. Another burial service.

April 24, 1912

Still dense fog prevailing, rendering further operations with the boats almost impossible. Noon. Another burial service held and seventy-seven bodies followed the others. The hoarse tone of the steam whistle reverberating through the mist, the dripping rigging and the ghostly sea, the heaps of the dead, and the hard, weather beaten faces of the crew, whose harsh voices join in the hymn tunefully rendered by Canon Hind, all combine to make a strange task stranger. Cold, wet, miserable and comfortless, all hands balance themselves against the heavy rolling of the ship as she lurches to the Atlantic swell, and even the most hardened must reflect on the hopes and fears, the dismay and despair, of those whose nearest and dearest, support and pride, have been wrenched from them by this tragedy.

April 26, 1912

The *Minia* joined us today in the work of recovery. Her first find was the body of Mr. Hays, the President of the Grand Trunk. A large amount of money and jewels have been recovered. The identification of most of the bodies has been established and details sent out for publication. It has been an arduous task for those who have had to overhaul and attend to the remains, the searching, the numbering, and identifying of each body. The embalmer is the only man to whom the work is pleasant, and I might add without undue exaggeration, enjoyable, for it is a labour of love, and the pride of doing a job well.

There was no refrigeration equipment on board, and because it took so long to find the bodies, many were in an advanced state of decomposition,

Body of *RMS Titanic* victim aboard the cable ship *Minia*
being made ready for makeshift coffin.
Public Archives of Nova Scotia, N-715.

and were buried at sea. Even in death social protocol was observed. Those bodies identified as being from third class were stacked in a heap on deck. Second class dead were sewn into canvas bags, and those from first class were laid out in coffins on the *Mackay-Bennett*'s poop deck. Of the 306 bodies recovered by the *Mackay-Bennett* 116 were buried at sea and the rest were brought to Halifax.

The Old Town clock on the harbour slope of the city's landmark Citadel Hill showed 9:00 a.m. on April 30 as the *Mackay-Bennett*, her flags flying at half-mast, sailed past the gracious Georgian mansions and manicured lawns of the seaport's South End towards the smoking chimneys of the North End. Crowds of people thronged the wharves and the tops of houses and buildings to watch it sail in. By 9:30 it had docked at wharf number four in the Canadian Naval Yards. The pier, just north of the present day-Angus L. Macdonald Bridge, could be secured from prying eyes behind stone walls and an iron gate. It was also close to the Mayflower Curling Club's new building which had just opened at 180 Agricola Street where the dead would be warehoused. The wharf was conveniently located near the North Street Railway Station where bodies were to be shipped by train.

Captain Fredrick Larnder told reporters the bodies "looked like swimmers asleep," but the *Daily Sketch* reported that of the 190 aboard, "116 were mutilated beyond recognition. Arms and legs were fractured and the features in many cases were so terribly cut and bruised that (it is declared) the injuries could not have been caused by the sea or wreckage, but must have resulted from a terrible explosion."

The bodies were brought to shore with the precision of a military operation. *The Halifax Herald* recorded the scene:

The sun shone brightly but there was nonetheless a species of darkness that could be felt from the time that the church and the fire bells began their solemn tolling, as the *Mackay-Bennett*, her afterdeck piled high with coffins and on her forward a hundred unshrouded bodies. Not more than a score of people saw the bodies carried off the ship to the pier by the bareheaded sailors who rapidly and silently transferred them to the big squad of undertakers. In less than five minutes after the first body was landed the initial hearse in a string of twenty started off for the extemporized morgue, the sentries at the gate for three long hours saluting with dreary monotony as the death carriages passed....Never before was the dockyard so carefully guarded, soldiers on the roofs of the departmental buildings within the walls and on every eminence patrolling with special instructions to stop every attempt at photography. In these efforts they were successful, so it is doubtful a single picture was taken.

The news editor at the *Halifax Chronicle*, Jim Hickey, was the only one who managed to breach the security. Before the *Mackay-Bennett* left Halifax Hickey had the foresight to make his own arrangements with Canon Hind for exclusive coverage. As the ship returned, Hickey hired a tugboat to meet the *Mackay-Bennett*. By prearranged agreement the Anglican clergyman threw down a bottle to Hickey containing a list of names of the identified dead on board. Hickey's story and the names were in print before even the coroner's office was informed.

Among the first of the bodies to be taken from the *Mackay-Bennett* directly to the CPR train station and shipped home was that of Hudson Allison. They found $143 in banknotes, $100 worth of travellers cheques, 15 pounds worth of gold, 35 British pounds and $4.40 in change in his pockets. His corpse was delivered to his brother in Montreal then taken to Chesterville, Ontario, where it was buried the next day in the rural cemetery near Winchester.

✓ John Snow and Company, the largest undertaking firm in the Maritimes was contracted to embalm the bodies. It subcontracted forty embalmers, including one woman, Annie O'Neill of New Brunswick, who handled all the females and children. The Mayflower Rink had been partitioned with curtains into a warren of sixty-seven cubicles so people could search for their loved ones with a modicum of privacy. The place smelled of formaldehyde and disinfectant. As grief-stricken relatives were taken through, attendants lifted the sheets to reveal the still forms. One of the undertakers, Frank Newell, was shocked to discover a distant relative among the dead, Arthur Newell, president of Boston's Fourth National Bank, who had been aboard the *Titanic* with his two daughters, both of whom survived.

The biggest shock, however, was reserved for Catherine Harbeck who arrived from Toledo only to be told that she couldn't be Mrs. Harbeck because Mrs. Harbeck had drowned in the sinking. Harbeck's body, the thirty-fifth recovered, was identified by his membership card in the Moving Picture and Projecting Machine Union that was found in his pocket. He died clutching a purse that belonged to Henriette Yrois, who had been registered as Harbeck's wife. Her body was not recovered, but inside her purse was Harbeck's wedding ring as well as 15 pounds in gold and 15 pounds in silver. His personal effects were given to his wife who took her husband's body back to Toledo for burial but never bothered to erect a headstone.

The most bizarre story involved Lydia Fox, who arrived from Rochester, New York, posing as her sister Cora to pick up her brother-in-law's body and $2,100 in personal effects on her sister's behalf. Before she could get away with it, Cora found out what Lydia was up to and intercepted her fraudulent scheme. Cora managed to get a telegram off to White Star representatives in Halifax just in time. The body was removed from the train in Truro and returned to Halifax, then shipped on to the widow in Rochester.

A rigorous system to identify the bodies had been devised by Nova Scotia's Deputy Registrar of deaths. Every effort was made to document whatever might help to identify the dead even after they were buried so no one would have to be exhumed. Each corpse was numbered as it was pulled from the sea and all personal effects were bagged. Identifying details were noted, and all the bodies photographed. Thomas McCaffry, for example, was number 292. The Records of Bodies and Effects estimated his age at fifty-three, noted his bald head and light mustache. The report says he was clad in a dress suit, brown overcoat, "T.C. Mc" embroidered on his drawers. Under Personal Effects are listed purse, knife, pocketbook, three studs, gold chain, locket, watch, pencil, sleeve links, pearl cuff links, ten pounds in British Bank notes, forty Italian Lira, nineteen shillings, and other coins.

McCaffry was returned to Montreal for burial in Notre-Dame-des-Neiges cemetery.

Halifax was crowded with the bereaved as prominent families from all over North American converged on the city. New York broker Maurice Rothschild came looking for the bodies of Mr. and Mrs. Isadore Strauss; Cape Breton senator David McKeen hoped to find Hugo Ross, H.G. Kelly; and the vice-president of the Grand Trunk Railway arrived to claim the body of Charles Hays.

The first of the funerals in Halifax, now dubbed by the papers, "City of the Dead," was held at the Anglican Cathedral Church of All Saints on May 1 for William Harrison, Bruce Ismay's private secretary. Hardly anyone knew it took place. "There were seven men in the cortege, including representatives of the local agency of the White Star Line. Neither organist nor choir was present—musical detail was not needed to make this funeral an impressive one," the *Halifax Evening Mail* reported. Harrison's was the 110th body recovered (green overcoat, dark suit, white shirt with blue stripes, and purple socks).

Two days later, Archbishop Edward McCarthy sang a requiem at St. Mary's Roman Catholic Cathedral. There were only four coffins in the church. At the time of the service no one knew who the dead—all female—were. They were identified as Catholics by their personal effects, which included rosaries and scapular medals. The church was packed with mourners, and according to the *Evening Mail*, it was an impressive service confident in its ceremony and ritual. "In its churchly shadow were to be noted many tear filled eyes," the *Mail* observed. During his sermon the rector paid tribute to the two priests who died on the *Titanic*. "One, Father Byles, was on the way to assist at the marriage of his brother, but instead he stayed and married souls to God. With the ship sinking slowly beneath them and the water lapping about their feet, the priests, (the other clergyman, Fr. Rev. Joseph Peruschitz, a Benedictine monk from Bavaria) were seen surrounded by passengers, performing their holy duties of office...."

Words of eulogy are unnecessary. When the priests stood on the sinking deck they were in their place beside their people. They died in priestly fashion. On duty. Theirs are but other names added to the long roll of priests who have maintained the splendid traditions of their calling...."

(In fact three Roman Catholic priests died on the *Titanic*; the third was Rev. Joseph Montrilia, a secular priest from Lithuania.)

The Catholics, nineteen of them, were buried in Mount Olivet Cemetery. All but four have been identified (see Appendix A).

Melancholy seized the city for the first week of May but there was no real outpouring of grief. Halifax was bathed in glorious spring sunshine, and the dead were so many strangers. The sense of loss among Haligonians was not as profound as if the dead had been friends and relatives. The curious turned out to gawk and perhaps pay their respects, but for the most part the crowds remained distant from the proceedings. A service for the Protestant dead was held at Brunswick Methodist Church in the afternoon of May 3. The pulpit was draped in purple and black and the sanctuary decorated with pink and white carnations "placed with careless care," a gift from Mrs. Hugh R. Rood, whose husband, a Seattle businessman, perished in the disaster. The band of the Royal Canadian Regiment played *Nearer My God to Thee* and the *Dead March from Saul*, then Clarence Mackinnon, principal of the Presbyterian College at Pine Hill delivered perhaps the most prescient and sublime of all the *Titanic* eulogies.

It is fitting that our words should be few and quiet in paying our tribute of respect to men whose deeds speak more eloquently than words," he said. "They shall rest quietly in our midst under the murmuring pines and hemlocks, but their story shall be told to our children and our to children's children.

There were no coffins present in the church. Most of the bodies were by now in an advanced state of decomposition. As the service for them was being conducted, fifty-nine were sent ahead to Fairview Lawn Cemetery, an eighteen-acre site on the outskirts of the city near Bedford Basin. The private non-denominational burial ground had only been open for eighteen years and no one had ever seen so many coffins together. Before the sexton could put the caskets in order for burial they were intercepted by a Rabbi M. Walter who had them all opened as they awaited interment. Initially, Walter had insisted that forty-four bodies in the morgue were Jewish. The coroner disagreed, however, and assigned only nine of them to the Baron de Hirsch Cemetery. Not satisfied with the coroner's ruling, Walter went through the coffins again as they sat on the ground at Fairview Cemetery and decided ten of the bodies were Jewish and commandeered them. When the five Protestant ministers arrived at 3 p.m. to preside over the graveside service they were shocked to discover the ten coffins missing. After two days of wrangling authorities refused to alter the burial permits so Rabbi Walter was ordered to return the bodies to Fairview Lawn Cemetery. The *Evening Mail* reported that "the coffins were somewhat damaged in the frequent changes to which they were subjected and it is said that someone will have to pay for new ones." Four of the nine bodies the rabbi declared to be those of Jews were, in the meantime, identified as Roman Catholics and consigned to Mount Olivet Cemetery instead. Ten bodies were interred in the Jewish Cemetery, but only two have been positively identified, those of Michel Navratil, a businessman from Nice who was kidnapping his children, Michel and Edmond from his estranged wife, and First Class Saloon Steward Frederick H. Wormald (see Appendix A).

(Navartil was in fact, a Catholic; he was presumed to be Jewish because he was travelling under the name of Hoffman. His children survived. When Wormald's widow and six children set out from Southampton to Nova Scotia three months after the sinking to visit the grave they were turned back by U.S. immigration authorities at Ellis Island and sent home without reaching Halifax.)

Those in Fairview Lawn were buried in three ranks (see Appendix A). Individual black granite headstones, each etched with the same date, April 15, 1912, were erected over all the graves later. The graves will be tended in perpetuity through a trust fund set up by the White Star Line, now administered by the City of Halifax. The most impressive tombstone was one paid for by Bruce Ismay. It was erected not to the memory of his secretary, William Harrison, but "to commemorate the long and faithful service" of the *Titanic*'s chief deck steward, Ernest Freeman. Why Freeman deserved so distinguished a monument is anybody's guess, but the inscription, presumably penned by Ismay himself, offers a clue: "He Remained at his post of duty, seeking to save others, Regardless of his own Life, and went down with the ship."

On Saturday, May 4, the most poignant of all the funeral services was held at St. George's Round Church for the unknown child. The crew of the *Mackay-Bennett* "adopted" the baby as its own, and took charge of the arrangements. The tiny white casket was smothered with floral tributes—wreaths shaped like stars, anchors, and a cross, and various sprays of carnations, roses, and lilies. The *Mackay-Bennett*'s entire complement, 75 officers and men, including Captain Larnder, attended, and six sailors acted as pallbearers. At the time, the boy was tentatively identified by a process of elimination as two-year-old Gösta Leonard Pålsson. He, his mother, and three siblings were on their way to Chicago to join their father. All were lost. If he is the Pålsson child, he lies by complete coincidence directly in front of his mother Alma's grave.

On May 6, the *Minia*, the second ship dispatched from Halifax to look for bodies brought back fifteen, among them the corpse of Charles Hays. The wireless operator aboard the *Minia*, Francis Dyke, wrote to his mother "The first (body) we picked up was C.M. Hayes (sic) of G. Trunk Rail. It was no trouble to identify him as he had a lot of papers on him and a watch with his name on." His coffin was brought back to Montreal aboard his private railway car, The Canada, which has been preserved and is on display at the Canadian Railway Museum at Delson, Quebec. There were simultaneous funeral services for Hays on May 8 at the American Presbyterian Church in Montreal and at the Church of St. Edmund King and Martyr in London, where he was eulogized as "a great man, not only of this hemisphere, but of the world." At precisely 11:30 a.m., five minutes of silence were observed not only in the American Presbyterian Church, but throughout the entire Grand Trunk network. As the *Herald* reported...

> From Montreal to Chicago, from New Brunswick to the Pacific
> coast, in all the thousands of miles of sidings and branch lines owned
> and operated by the Grand Trunk Railway, in every Grand Trunk
> Depot, at every Grand Trunk Crossing, action ceased for the space
> of five full minutes as the Grand Trunk system paid its final respects
> to the memory of its great departed chief, Charles Melville Hays.
> For five minutes activities were suspended, and the thousands of
> individuals who serve the great system in various capacities bowed
> their heads in silent tribute. Then once more, work resumed, the
> wheels turned and in thirty seconds things were as they had been
> before.

The 39th Psalm was read, the congregations sang *Nearer My God to Thee*, and a memorial plaque was unveiled in both churches, but when the American Presbyterian Church was torn down in 1934, it disappeared. Hays is buried in the Pine Hill section of Mount Royal Cemetery. A massive granite monument was erected over the grave. Carved into the back of it are the words, now obscured by overgrown shrubs: "And so he died, and the example of his simple devoted consecrated life is our priceless heritage. We are a different people and we are a better people because this man lived and worked and loved and died." Eventually a railway divisional point in Saskatchewan, Melville, and the town of Hays in Alberta were named after him. A statue to him was erected in Prince Rupert, B.C.

The remains of George Graham, body number 147, clad in a "black overcoat; blue serge suit," were delivered to his brother in St. Mary's, Ontario. The funeral, one of the largest ever seen in Harriston, was on May 6. A special train from Toronto made up of five coaches, including The Eatonia, the private car of J.C. Eaton, arrived at the CPR station at 11 a.m., and according to the St. *Mary's Journal*, the coffin was transported to the Methodist Church.

"The special train had on board some fifty representatives of the Eaton

Company...the floral tributes were very beautiful and required special conveyances. All business in the town was suspended during the funeral service and the town flag was at half-mast." Graham was initially buried in the cemetery in Harriston, but in 1933, his wife exhumed the body and moved it to the cemetery in St. Mary's.

On Friday, May 10, the last four bodies that had been stored at the Mayflower Curling Rink in Halifax were disposed of. One was shipped to his home in Norway and the three others buried with the rest of the *Titanic*'s victims in Fairview. Valuables removed from the 209 bodies brought to Halifax were said to be worth a quarter of a million dollars, and the unclaimed bullion, currency, gems, and coins were turned over to the Provincial Secretary of Nova Scotia, then shipped to the White Star Line in New York.

In Winnipeg a memorial plaque to the six local *Titanic* victims was unveiled in City Hall. Today it is in the passageway that links the old administration building to the new council chambers. It reads: Erected by the People of Winnipeg in memory of Mark Fortune, John Hugh Ross, Thomson Beattie, Charles A. Fortune, George E. Graham, J.J. Borebank. They with 1,484 others died when the *S.S. Titanic* foundered in the mid-Atlantic, April 15, 1912. They died that women and children may live.

Streets in Winnipeg were named after each of the dead men and the Fortune family donated the memorial chimes which still peal each Sunday in Knox United Church to the memory of Mark and Charles.

Joseph Fynney was laid to rest in Montreal's Mount Royal Cemetery. Fynney left one-quarter of his estate, almost a thousand pounds, to Alfred Gaskell's family as their compensation for the death of his under-aged travelling companion. Which is why, perhaps, carved into his modest tombstone are the words "his delight was in doing good."

Harry Molson's body was never recovered. His family placed an appropriate bronze memorial to him in Montreal's Mount Royal Cemetery with the epitaph: Psalm 77, Verse 19, "Thy way is in the sea, and Thy path in the great waters, and Thy footsteps are not known."

A third ship, the *Montmagny*, which had been dispatched from Halifax to do a final sweep of the ocean, came across debris, including a part of the *Titanic*'s deck, "polished and white painted wood," and on May 10 picked up an oak newel post. The *Montmagny* found four bodies, those of steerage passenger Harold Reynolds, the young baker with a Toronto address in his pocket (807 Yonge Street), clinging to a life preserver; a fifteen-year-old unidentified Syrian girl; one of the ship's stewards; and an unidentified crewman. The crewman was buried at sea and the three others were dropped off at Louisbourg, Nova Scotia and shipped by train to Halifax for burial.

On May 15, the Newfoundland-based steamer, *Algerine*, recovered the body of saloon steward James McGrady. His was the last of the 150 victims to be buried in Halifax.

One full month after the disaster, the *Oceanic* came across a life raft bobbing at 47°01' N; 30°56' W., 200 miles southeast of where the *Titanic* sank. It was Collapsible A. Aboard were the three bodies which had been set adrift. Thomson Beattie's corpse was "advanced far in decomposition." He had died in formal dress, and was identified by papers in his overcoat. There was also a firefighter and a steward dead in the boat. "There was no evidence to show whether or not the three men had perished either from cold or hunger, or not," said one newspaper account. "Their positions showed only that they had died resignedly, perhaps while unconscious. The strong presumption was that they had died from exposure."

Sir Shane Leslie, who was aboard the *Oceanic* that day, recalled that the sea was calm at noon when the watch called out that "something could be seen floating ahead. The ship slowed down and it was apparent that object was an open lifeboat floating in the mid Atlantic. What was horrifying was that it contained three prostrate figures. Orders from the bridge dispatched a lifeboat with an officer and a medical officer. What followed was ghastly. Two sailors could be seen, their hair bleached by exposure to sun and salt, and a third figure wearing full evening dress flat on the benches. All three were dead and the bodies had been tossing on the Atlantic swell under the open sky ever since it had seen the greatest of ocean liners sink. The boat was full of ghastly souvenirs, such as rings and watches and even children's shoes from those who had been unrescued and had been consigned to the ocean one by one."

The three bodies were carefully sewn into canvas bags with a steel bar at the foot of each. Then, one after the other, the body bags splashed into the sea, and the Atlantic entombed the last of the *Titanic*'s victims. In a phenomenal example of what might be described as cosmic serendipity, Beattie's body was buried at sea on his mother's birthday almost at the same spot in the Atlantic where she had been born eighty-two years earlier.

Thomson Beattie.
Courtesy of Robert A. Stevens.

Chapter Fifteen

THOSE WHO SURVIVED the sinking of the *Titanic* behaved as if they were members of some secret fraternity, who, in the aftermath of the disaster, distanced themselves from their sorrowful initiation. As charges and counter-charges began to fly back and forth it seemed as if most of the survivors had taken a vow not to talk about what they had been through.

There was no doubt Bruce Ismay and Captain Smith had been negligent, but those who were on the ship did not, for the most part, wish to publicly apportion blame. When pressed to sue the White Star Line for damages, Clara Hays, for example, refused. "When one is a guest (of Bruce Ismay), one does not sue one's host," she said imperiously.

The women simply wanted to forget. For the longest time no one dared asked them what happened that night. No one wore their survivors' badge proudly.

Major Arthur Peuchen was one of the exceptions. From the moment he set foot on land, Peuchen accused Captain Smith of "carelessness, gross carelessness." In countless interviews Peuchen said the same thing. "The Captain knew we were going into an ice field, and why should he remain dining in the saloon when such danger was about? Less mother of pearl and a searchlight on the bow could have saved hundreds of lives," he thundered.

Peuchen was no fool. He knew he would have to justify his being saved, and protect his reputation. So even before the *Carpathia* reached New York, Peuchen had Lightoller sign a certificate that stated he had been pressed into service. Peuchen took the precaution, he said, because he didn't want people to think him a coward. "Married women were envious when they saw that I, a strong man, had been saved while their husbands, sons and brothers had gone down."

Peuchen said he thought it was only right that he have the piece of paper because the quartermaster in charge, Robert Hitchens was a total incompetent. "He was not fit to be a common seaman. He was a cowardly man who knew nothing about navigation. He wanted to know if we spotted any buoys. Fancy, buoys in the middle of the Atlantic," Peuchen fumed. "He saw all kinds of things, and my conclusion was that he had been drinking."

Peuchen was the only Canadian subpoenaed to appear before the U.S. Senate investigation into the disaster. He was summoned to give testimony in Washington on Tuesday, April 23. Neither American nor British, the major proved to be one of the most credible, impartial, expert witnesses. He tempered much of his criticism before committee chairman Senator Alden Smith, but was vehement in his indictment of seamanship aboard the *Titanic*. "I might say I was rather surprised that the sailors were not at their stations as I have seen fire drill very often on steamers where they all stand at attention, so many men at the bow and the stern of the lifeboats," he told the inquiry, "They seemed to be short of sailors around the lifeboats." Peuchen's assessment was scathing. "I imagine this crew was what we would call in yachting terms, a scratch crew, brought from different vessels. They might be the best, but they were not accustomed to working together."

Peuchen also had a lot to say about the lack of leadership and the lackadaisical attitude among the crew that left passengers with a false sense of security.

"There was no alarm sounded whatever," he complained, "In fact I talked with two young ladies who claimed to have had a very narrow escape. They said...they were not awakened."

Senator Smith: They were not awakened?

Maj. Peuchen: They slept through the crash.

Senator Smith: I think you said that from your judgement and from your observation there was no general alarm given?

Maj Peuchen: No I did not hear one. I was around the boat all the time.

His testimony was cogent, forceful, and crucial. Senator Smith was grateful for Peuchen's appearance, but in Toronto, Peuchen was maligned for being too self-satisfied. The *Toronto Mail* discredited Peuchen "because he talked too much."

"He put himself in the position of a man who had to defend himself before the necessity for the defence was apparent." No one quite believed Peuchen's version of how he got off the ship, and he was ridiculed because he survived. "He said he was a yachtsman to get himself off the ship," was one taunt about him that circulated, "And if it had been a fire, he would have said he was a fireman." More malicious gossips would claim the Major was a coward who had dressed as a woman to save his skin. When World War I broke out in 1914, Peuchen retired from Standard Chemical to command the Home Battalion of the Queen's Own.

After the war he discovered his social standing in Toronto still was stained because now he had survived both the war and the sinking of the *Titanic*. He lost much of his money in the 1920s as the result of bad investments and he spent the last four years of his life living in his company's dormitory in Hinton, Alberta. Peuchen was exonerated somewhat in 1935 when Lightoller published his memoirs in which he wrote that Peuchen had been unfairly criticized for carrying out what was a direct order. By then it was too late. Arthur Peuchen had been dead for six years. He died in Toronto at the age of seventy on December 7, 1929.

The bereaved got on with their lives as best they could. Margaret Wright married in Oregon as planned but she took time to write to Dr. Pain's family in Hamilton the day after the wedding.

How your poor heart must be torn to lose Alfred as you have in his prime and in such perfect health. We did not really get acquainted until the Friday we sailed so though I knew him for but three days I felt he was a friend. He said I was the first lady he had ever spoken to. He had seemed so good getting up games for the young fellows on board. We had several meals together and he told me how much he had enjoyed his stay in England. … It is such a grief to me that I did not say goodbye to him, but I thought, as everyone else did, that we would back to the *Titanic* before long. When the awful news came to us that only 700 were saved, how grieved I felt and how I wished your son had been among the 700. It all seems so sad and overwhelming. My mind will never forget it as long as I live. I trust just these few lines may comfort the heart of Dr. Pain's sorrow-stricken mother is my prayer, with much sympathy...

After Thomson Beattie's body was found in a lifeboat a full month after the disaster, Maud MacArthur sent a letter to Beattie's sister, Christine. It is not clear whether MacArthur was trying to console the family or convince herself that she had a relationship with Beattie.

"Thomson and I were more to one another than merely friends, although I would never acknowledge it until later, even to myself," MacArthur wrote.

He has been the love of my life. I have always had a great deal of attention from men (please do not think I mean it in a conceited way) and have not been particularly anxious to settle down—and so we drifted along. Thomson of course was perfectly willing things should be as they were for reasons of his own ....This trip he had been so terribly longing for me, every letter being full of how he was enjoying himself, but of how much more he would have enjoyed it had I been with him. I am telling you all of this because that is a side of Thomson's character I don't think his family knew about. He never paid the slightest attention to any girl in Winnipeg but me, and never until this past winter did he acknowledge he was jealous of other men's attentions.

Of course the last three days have been terribly hard on me. Fancy my darling boy being on that raft and dying almost immediately after from I suppose exhaustion—it nearly drives me mad to think of it. I have had many wires from New York and the White Star people are sending me his watch which was found on him. It was a little cheap one he got in Venice. I am afraid some unscrupulous person must have taken his wallet for I am sure when he went down he would put it in his pocket. You know he had on his dinner jacket?

This letter may bore you and I may have told you the same things over and over again but my mind is full of him and what I have been told of him on his trip and I know you will forgive me. If only I could have kissed him goodbye and we could have had one last talk on this earth, but to have him taken from me in such a terrible manner, it is too awful.

One morning in late June, 1912, when the sky was crisp and blinding blue, and pastures in the Ottawa Valley were lush green and filled with the scent of lilacs, Hudson Allison's brother, Percy, received an unexpected delivery. Two dozen Clydesdales were waiting for him at the train station in Winchester. The horses that Hud had shipped by tramp steamer from Scotland had arrived. As Percy drove them to the farm, they thundered down a rural road that ran by Maple Grove cemetery, past the towering obelisk, solid and splendid, that marks Hudson Allison's grave, and left it behind in a trail of dust.

The Allison family monument, Maple Grove cemetery,
Ottawa Valley.
Photo by Alan Hustak.

Afterword

PAUL CHEVRÉ, who spent each summer for fourteen years in Canada crossed the Atlantic one final time to get home to France and never sailed again. He died in Paris on February 20, 1914, at the age of forty-seven. "Paul Chevré was a passenger on the ill-fated *Titanic*, and although he survived the shock, it is doubtful he ever fully recovered from it," read his obituaries in the Montreal papers. They concluded with the observation: "It is said that he dreaded the return voyage to France."

HÉLÈNE LANAUDIÈRE-CHAPUT BAXTER, Quigg's mother, died in her suite in the Drummond Apartments in Montreal in June, 1923. She was sixty-one.

TREVOR ALLISON, the baby who survived, died of food poisoning at the age of seventeen in August 1929, during a vacation in Maine. He was buried next to the father he never knew in Maple Ridge cemetery between Winchester and Chesterville, Ontario. Allison's estate was left to his brothers, and the fortune was lost in the stock market crash.

ZETTE DOUGLAS' marriage to Dr. Douglas deteriorated. She contracted a mild case of polio and for awhile required a leg brace to get around. Her husband became an alcoholic, lost his hospital privileges in Montreal, and eventually moved to Sherbrooke. Zette waited until after her mother's death in 1923 to file for a divorce. In those days divorce proceedings in Canada involved a humiliating public hearing before a Canadian Senate Committee and a special act of the Canadian Parliament before the decree was final. She later lived with a Westmount stockbroker, Edgar Cole Richardson. Together they moved to Redlands, California, to a house at 715 West Clark St. There, according to a nephew, Zette spent her days surrounded "by mothballs and memories." By the time she died of a heart attack on New Year's Eve, 1954, there was almost nothing left of the Baxter estate. She bequeathed all her household furnishings to her family in

Mabel Fortune in later years.
Courtesy of Mrs. Robert Driscoll.

Montreal, but Richardson was unable to carry out her wishes. "Times have not been good to us," he wrote to her beneficiaries in Montreal, "and I am afraid I cannot pay the transportation cost or customs charges. Incidentally, there is no market in California for her effects."

BERTHE MAYNÉ stayed in Montreal for a few months then returned to Paris where she resumed her career as a singer. She settled in the Brussels suburb of Bercham-Ste-Agathe. In her old age she was much like old Rose in the Cameron movie. She tried to persuade her nephew that she had been aboard the *Titanic* going to Canada with a young millionaire, but he didn't believe her. It was only after she died on October 11, 1962, and relatives found a shoe box full of clippings among her belongings, that the identity of the mysterious Madame de Villiers was at last revealed.

HILDA SLAYTER was married as planned to Henry Reginald Dunbar Lacon on Denman, Island, B.C., June 1, 1912. Their son, Reginald William Beecroft Lacon, distinguished himself in the Royal Canadian Navy. She spent the rest of her life on the west coast and died there in 1965.

MARY FORTUNE lived in Winnipeg until she moved to Toronto to live with Ethel where she died on March 8, 1929.

ETHEL FORTUNE married her fiancé, Crawford Gordon, in 1913. Seven years later they moved to Jamaica and then to London, England in 1931 when her husband was appointed manager of the Bank of Commerce. Their first-born, Crawford Gordon Jr. became the head of A.V. Roe, that in the 1950s produced Canada's legendary Avro Arrow, the world's most advanced military aircraft.

MABEL FORTUNE married jazz musician Harrison Driscoll in spite of her parents' wishes. They had a son, Robert, but soon afterwards Mabel fell for the charms of a female suitor from Ottawa, Charlotte Armstrong. Mabel left her husband, put her son in boarding school, and moved with Charlotte to Victoria where she lived until her death on February 19, 1968.

ALICE FORTUNE married insurance broker Charles Holden Allen and they lived in Montreal for most of their lives. The Allens had a vacation home in Chester, Nova Scotia, where she died. She and her husband liked Chester so much they are buried in the local cemetery.

CLARA HAYS spent more time at her summer house on Cushing Island, Maine, than she did in Montreal. "For the last five years of her life, Granny always went back to the sea," her grandaughter recalled. "All the time we were at the table all she talked about was the sea." She died in 1955 at the age of ninety-six.

ORIAN HAYS Davidson married her husband's business partner, stockbroker Robert Hickson in 1924 and died in Montreal in 1979 when she was ninety-three.

ANNE PERREAULT, her maid, married a man named Pickett and moved to California where they ran a gas station in the middle of the desert. She was ninety when she died on November 18, 1968.

MATHILDA WEISZ married Edward Lancelot Wren in the spring of 1914 and in an interview with her on the twentieth anniversary of the sinking of the *Titanic*, the *Montreal Herald* reported she had raised $57,000 for charity, singing, during World War I and for her efforts had been awarded the Medaille de la Reine Elisabeth by the King of Belgium. She died in Montreal on October 13, 1953 at the age of seventy-nine and is buried in an unmarked grave in Montreal's Notre-Dames-des-Neiges Cemetery.

BERT DICK, like Major Peuchen, was ostracized simply because he survived. In Calgary it was said he dressed as a woman to save his life. His name was so tarnished by the gossip that Dick's hotel business suffered. He sold it, but continued to make money in real estate. Vera studied music at the Royal Conservatory in Toronto and was a well-known vocalist in Calgary. The Dicks lived in the fashionable Mount Royal neighbourhood. An elaborate brick staircase in the front of their house is still referred to as the *Titanic* staircase because it was patterned after the Grand staircase. Bert died in 1970 at the age of eighty; Vera died in Banff in 1973.

NESHAN KREKORIAN made it to Brantford, Ontario, and spent a month recuperating from a bout of pneumonia. He moved to St. Catharines in 1918, and married. The *Titanic* voyage was his first and only time on the water. He never again went near a boat. Whenever he went with his family to a beach or saw a large body of water, his daughter said, his face betrayed his thoughts. "He would gaze at the water, and instantly you knew he was reliving that night." Krekorian died May 21, 1978.

EVA HART never married. Deported back to England, she embarked on successful careers as a singer, social welfare officer, and a court magistrate. She was made an MBE in 1974. She didn't get to Winnipeg, where she was bound as a child, until 1980, when she visited as a delegate to a convention. In 1992, she attended the premiere of the IMAX film *Titanica* at the Museum of Civilization in Hull, Que. She died February 15, 1996.

The COUNTESS OF ROTHES lost her husband in 1925 and married Col. Claude Macfie. She had a boat named after her to commemorate her heroism. Years after the disaster, while dining with friends, she became ill suddenly and realized it was because the string quartet in the room was playing the *Tales of Hoffman* which she had last heard at dinner on the *Titanic*. She died on September 12, 1956.

ANTOINETTE MALLET returned to France with her son to live with her in-laws. Like Alice Cleaver, and a number of other passengers, no one knows what eventually became of her.

Some of those who survived the sinking moved to Canada years after the disaster.

BRIDGET DELIA BRADLEY a third class passenger who had left Kingwilliamstown, County Cork, for America, married a Canadian, Bernard LaSha from Gananoque, Ontario, in 1926. They had four children, and one of her daughters wrote her biography, *Unsinkable Bridget*. In 1953, Mrs. LaSha was persuaded to see the first movie, *Titanic*, "She hesitated about wanting to see it, but with a little persuasion we managed to get her to go. She became very emotional during the movie and at times kept shaking her head as if to say 'It didn't happen that way.'" After the movie she was introduced on stage and later that evening had her picture taken with the mayor and the manager of the theatre. She was given a bouquet of flowers and a lifetime pass to the theatre which she never used. "For once in her life," her daughter recalled, "she was in the spotlight, if only for such a short time." She died on January 24, 1956, and is buried in St. John's Roman Catholic Cemetery in Gananoque, Ontario.

MARIANA ASSAF made a small fortune for herself in Ottawa, then returned to Syria.

Four of the survivors, first class stewardess Emma Bliss, Assistant Chef John Collins (who was swept overboard with a child in his arms when the ship sank), Mrs. Elizabeth Mellinger, and her daughter Madeline Mann, met for a *Titanic* reunion dinner at the Royal York Hotel in Toronto on April 15, 1939. The Fortune sisters and the Dicks in Calgary declined the invitation. Privately, they were appalled. At the time The *Toronto Star* reported "it is planned that this meeting might be the nucleus for a world-wide *Titanic* association" but the majority of those who survived were not interested in remembering the disaster.

In 1940, a woman by the name of Loraine Kramer made headlines when she claimed to be Loraine Allison. She claimed that Thomas Andrews didn't go down with the ship, but survived, rescued her, and went into hiding. As preposterous as her claims were, Kramer harassed the Allison family for her share of the estate for the next ten years. Not that there was much at stake. Most of the estate had been lost through bad investments even before Trevor died, and the rest was lost during the Depression.

In 1953, the *Titanic* was given a fresh life when the movie with Clifton Webb and Barbara Stanwyk came out and won an Academy Award for its screenplay. Soon after, Walter Lord's classic, *A Night to Remember*, was published. Around the same time a woman in Montreal claimed to be a survivor and dined out on the story of how her two children floated away on the iceberg that sank the ship.

The Maritime Museum of the Atlantic in Halifax opened a modest *Titanic* display in 1982. Enlarged in 1998, it features a deck chair and some of the hand-carved panelling from the First Class Lounge. The discovery of the wreck by Canadian marine scientist Robert Ballard on September 1, 1985, stimulated public interest as never before.

As late as 1989, the CBC was duped into carrying an interview with a man named Bill Muller who claimed he was the "last survivor" of the *Titanic*. Muller purported to be a valet to a German banker on the ship, but neither Muller nor the banker were on board.

BERTHA WATT, who was twelve-years-old and on her way with her mother from Scotland to Oregon, married a Vancouver dentist, Leslie Marshall, in 1923, and became a Canadian citizen. She spent the rest of her life in Vancouver. The last Canadian survivor, she died on March 4, 1993.

Appendix A

FAIRVIEW LAWN CEMETERY

Rice, John Reginald
Giles, Ralph
Marriot, J.W.
Price, Ernest
Palsson, Alma
Poggi, E.
Shillaber, Charles
White, Arthur
Marsh, Frederick
Butt, Robert, First Class Steward
Talbot, George Frederick
Allen, Henry
Roberts, Edward James W.
Wellesley, Henry
Davies, Robert J.
Cave, Herbert
King, Alfred
Matherson, Davies
White, J.
Roberts, F.
Reeves, F.
Sawyer, Frederick
Everett, Thomas James
Givard, Hans Christensen
Johansson, Gustav Joel
Teuton, Thomas Moore
Donati, Italo
Elliot, Everett Edward
Cartwright, James Edward
Storey, Thomas
Freeman, Ernest Edward
Kvillner, Johan Henrik
Howell, Arthur Albert
Stanbrooke, Augustus
Wittman, Henry
Unknown
Alphonse, Meo

Thomas, A. Mullin
King, Ernest Waldron
Zakarian, Maprieder
Andersen, Albert Karvin
Chapman, John Henry
Johanson, Jakob Alfred
Hodges, Henry Price
Hutchison, J.
Johnsson, Malkolm Joachim
Sather, Simon Sivertsen
Gatti, Luigi

[SECOND ROW]

Norman, Robert Douglas,
Baxter, Thomas Ferguson
Lefevre, George
Ingram, G.
Wareham, Robert Arthur
Grodidge, Ernest Edward
Goree, Frank
Dean, George H.
Fellows, J. Alfred
Holloway, Sidney
McQuillan, William
Unknown
Unknown
Unknown
Unknown
Allaria, Baptiste Antonia
Akerman, Joseph Francis
Brown, J.
Hosgood, Richard
Carney, William
Dawson, J.
Bailey, George Francis
Bristow, Robert C.
Couch, Frank,
Dashwood, William G.
Cox, William Denton
Wooford, F.
Unknown
Shea, John

Swane, George
Waelens, Achille

[THIRD ROW]

Pålsson, Gösta Leonard, the "unknown" child
Harrison, William Henry
Deeble, Alfred
Butler, Reginald Fenton
Samuel, O.W.
Unknown
Hume, John Law
Unknown
Unknown
Unknown
Unknown
Unknown
Franklin, Alan Vincent
Unknown
Stone, Edward F.
May, Arthur William
Unknown
Unknown
Unknown
Unknown
Unknown
Unknown
Unknown
Unknown
Unknown
Bogie, Leslie Norman
Unknown
Unknown
Unknown
Unknown
Unknown
Henriksson, Jenny Louisa
Smith, Charles
Unknown
Unknown
Heininen, Wendla Maria
Deslands, Percival

[There are five graves between the second and the third rows.]

McGrady, James
Reynolds, Harold
Wicklund, Jacob Alfred
McCrae, Arthur Gaidan
Unknown

MOUNT OLIVET ROMAN CATHOLIC CEMETERY

Ali, William
Bernard, Baptiste
Clarke, John Frederick P.
DeBreucq, Maurice Emil
Hanna, Mansour
Hendekovic, Ignaz
Jaillet, Henri
Lemberopoulos, Peter
Linhart, Wenzel
Morgan, Thomas
Ovies y Rodriguez, Servando
Piasso, Pomeo
Rice, Margaret
Unknown
Unknown
Unknown
Unknown
Youssif, Gerios
Zabour, Hileni

BARON DE HIRSCH JEWISH CEMETERY

Navratil, Michel
Unknown
Unknown
Unknown
Unknown
Unknown
Unknown
Unknown
Unknown
Wormald, Frederick H.

Appendix B

THE *TITANIC*'S CANADA-BOUND PASSENGERS
[Those whose names are in bold type did not survive]

[First Class]

Allison, Bess Waldo Daniels, b. November 14, 1886.
Allison, Joshua Creighton b. December 9, 1881, married on his birthday in Milwaukee, Wisconsin, in 1907. They had two children,
Allison, Helen Loraine, b June 5, 1909 and,
Allison, Hudson Trevor, b. May 7, 1911, survived the sinking of the *Titanic* and died of food poisoning during a holiday in Maine on August 7, 1929.
Beattie, Thomson, b. November 25, 1875.
Baxter, Quigg Edmond, b. Montreal, July 13, 1887.
Baxter, Hélène Chaput, d. Montreal, June 19, 1923.
Borebank, John James, b. 1870, West Hallan, Derbyshire.
Colley Edward Pomery, b. Kildare, April 15, 1875.
Chevré, Paul Romain, b. 1867, d. February 20, 1914.
Cherry Gladys
Cleaver, Alice
Daniels, Sarah
Davidson, Orian Hays, b. November 18, 1884, d. Montreal, May 3, 1979.
Dick, Albert Adrian, b. Winnipeg, July 29, 1880, d. September 8, 1970
Dick, Vera, b. 1894, d. Banff, October 7, 1973.
Douglas, Zette, Mary Hélène, b. April 4, 1885, d. December 31, 1954.
Dyer-Edwards, Lucy Noel Martha, The Countess of Rothes, b. December 25, 1878, she remarried Col. Claude Macfie after the count died.
d. September 12, 1956.
Fortune, Mark, b. 1847, and his wife,
Fortune, Mary, b. May 12, 1851, died in Toronto on March 8, 1929, and their children:
Fortune, Ethel Flora, b. Sept. 22, 1883, married Crawford Gordon, died in Toronto, March 21, 1961.
Fortune, Alice, b. May 10, 1887, married Charles Allen, d. April 8, 1961.
Fortune, Mabel Helen, b. November 3, 1888, d. February 19, 1968.
Fortune, Charles, b. October 13, 1892.
Graham, George, b. June 11, 1873, St. Mary's Ontario.
Hays, Charles Melville, b. May 16, 1856.
Hays, Clara, b. October 13, 1859, d. Montreal, February 1, 1955.

Lesneur, Gustave, from Ottawa, was travelling in one of the *Titanic*'s two millionaires' suites, rooms B-51-53-55, as a servant employed by the Cardeza family from Philadelphia. Thomas Cardeza, an explorer and an art collector was with his mother.

Mayné, Bertha, b. 21 July 1887, Ixelles, Belgium, d. Berchem-Saint-Agathe, Belgium, October 11, 1962.

McCaffry, Thomas b. 1866.

Molson, Harry Markland, b. Montreal, August 9, 1856.

Maloni, Ruberta

Partner, Austen, b. 1871

Payne, Vivian b. 1889

Perrault, Anne

Peuchen, Arthur Godfrey, b. Montreal, April 19, 1859, d. Toronto, December 7, 1929.

Ross, Hugo John b. Nov. 24, 1875.

Wright, George. b. Tufts Cove, Nova Scotia, 1849.

[SECOND CLASS]

Bliss, Emma, d. June 19, 1959 in Toronto.

Brown, Mildred

Fynney, Joseph b. 1876.

Gaskell, Alfred b. 1896.

Hart, Benjamin b. December 25, 1864.

Hart, Esther, b May 13, 1865.

Hart, Eva b. January 31, 1905, d. February 14, 1996.

Harbeck, William, b. 1863.

Hickman, Leonard, b. 1887.

Hickman, Lewis, b. 1879.

Hickman, Stanley, b. 1890.

Kirkland, Rev. Charles

Levy, René-Jacques

Mallet, Albert

Mallet, André

Mallet, Antoinette

Maybery, Frank, b. 1872.

McCrie, James Matthew

Mellinger, Elizabeth Anne Maidment, b. June 1, 1870, Walthanstowe, England, emigrated to Canada with her daughter, Madeline, in 1913, d. January 4, 1962, buried in St. John's Ridgeway cemetery near Welland, Ontario.

Mellinger, Madeline Violet, Mann, b, February 22, 1899, emigrated to Canada with her mother. m. David Daniel Mann, d. May 27, 1976 in Toronto.

Norman, Robert Douglas, b. 1884.

Pain, Dr. Arthur, b. 1888 in Hamilton, Ontario.

Richard, Emile

Slayter, Hilda, b. April 5, 1882, d. April 12, 1965.

Swane, George, b. 1885.

Sjöstedt, Ernst Adolf, b. Hjo, Sweden, September 9, 1852.

Wright, Marion, b. May 26, 1885, d. July 4, 1965.

Weisz, Leopold

Weisz, Matilda, d. October 13, 1953.

Watt, Elizabeth Ingles Watt, b. 1872, d. September 18, 1951.

Watt, Bertha, b. September 11, 1899, m. Dr. Leslie Marshall, 1921, d. March 4, 1993. They are buried in Fraserview Cemetery, New Westminister, B.C.

Yrois, Henriette

[THIRD CLASS]

Andersson, Alfrida Konstantia, b. December 25, l872.

Andersson, Ebba Iris Alfrida, b. November 14, 1905.

Andersson, Johan, b. January 21, 1873.

Andersson, Ellis Anna Maria, b. January 19, 1910.

Andersson, Ingeborg Constancia, b. April 16, 1902.

Andersson, Sigrid Elizabeth, b. April 16, 1900.

Andersson, Sigvard Harald Elias, b. July 21, 1908.

Assaf, Mariana

Assaf, Gerios

Boulous, Sultani

Boulous, Akar

Boulous, Hannah

Boulous, Nourelain

Bradley, Bridget Delia LaSha, b. Kingwilliamstown, County Cork, Ireland, January 10, 1890, d. January 24, 1956, Gananoque, Ontario.

Braund, Lewis Richard, b.1883.

Braund, Owen Harris, b. 1889.

Colbert, Patrick b. Abbeyfale, Nov. 5, 1887.

Danbom, Ernest, b. Oct 26 1877

Danbom Gilber b. Nov 16 1911.

Danbom, Sigrid, b. March 10 1884.

Garfith, John, b. 1889.

Gerios, Assaf

Gerios, Youssef

Hanna, Mansour
Kallio, Nikolai, b. 1895.
Khalil, Maria Elias
Khalil, Solomon
Krekorian, Neshan, b. May 12, 1886, d. May 21, 1978.
Maenpaad, Matti, b. 1890.
Mardirosian, Sarkis
Morrow, Thomas Rowan, b. April 26, 1880.
Nicola-Yarred, Elias
Nicola-Yarred, Jemil
Nirva, Isak, b. 1870.
Nirva, Maija Lisa?
Novel, Mansour
O'Sullivan, Bridgit Mary, b. County Cork, Ireland, May 18, 1890.
Patchett, George, b. 1893.
Reynolds, Harold, b. 1891.
Rintamaki, Matti, b. 1877
Sirayanian, Orsen
Sage, George, b. 1892.
Vartunian, David
Wiklund, Karl Johan, b. 1883.
Wiklund, Jacob Alfred, b.1886.
Wiseman, Phillipe
Zarkarian, Maprieder
Zarkarian, Ortin
Zimmerman, Leo

[CREW]

Collins, John
William Edwy Ryerson, b. Port Dover, Ontario, 1878, d. December 9, 1949.

Selected Bibliography

Ballard, Robert D., *The Discovery of the Titanic*, Viking, 1987.

Beesley, Lawrence, *The Loss of the S.S. Titanic*, Houghton Mifflin, 1912.

Brinnin, John Malcolm, *Sway of the Grand Saloon*, Delacorte, 1971.

Coleman, Terry, *The Liners*, Penguin, 1976.

Davie, Michael, *Titanic: The Full Story of a Tragedy*, Grafton Books, 1983.

Eaton, John P. and Charles Haas, *Titanic, Triumph and Tragedy* by W.W. Norton, 1986.

Gracie, Archibald, *The Truth About the Titanic*, M. Kennerley, 1913.

Hyslop, Donald, Alastair Forsyth and Sheila Jemina, *Titanic Voices: Memoirs from the Fateful Voyage*, St. Martin's Press, 1998.

LaSha, M. *Unsinkable Bridgit*. Privately printed, 1968.

Lightoller, Chas., *Titanic and Other Ships*, Nicholson and Watson, 1935.

Lord, Walter, *A Night to Remember*, Bantam, 1955.

Lord, Walter, *The Night Lives On*, William Morrow, 1986.

Lynch, Don and Ken Marschall, *Titanic: An Illustrated History*, Viking/Madison, 1992.

Marcus, Geoffrey, *The Maiden Voyage*, Viking, 1969.

O'Leary, Grattan, *Recollections of People, Press and Politics*, Macmillan Canada, 1977.

Padfield, Peter, *The Titanic and the Californian*, John Day, 1965.

Pratt, E.J. "Titanic," *Collected Poems*, 1958.

Sloper, William T. *The Life and Times of Andrew Jackson Sloper*. Privately printed, 1949.

Stewart C., *Crawford Gordon: His Fast Life and Times*, McGraw Hill, 1998.

The Titanic Disaster Hearings, Official Transcripts of the 1912 U.S. Subcommittee of the Committee on Commerce.

Wreck Commissioners' Court Proceedings Before the Rt. Hon. Lord Mersey on a Formal Investigation Ordered by the British Board of Trade into the Loss of the S.S. Titanic, 1912.

Wynn Craig Wade, *Titanic, End of a Dream*, Penguin, 1976.

Index

Visit us on the Web
http://www.cam.org/~vpress